Uncovering Student Thinking
About **Mathematics**
in the **Common Core**

Grades K–2

To my mother and grandfather, Karen Bradstreet and James Gangi, whose belief in me continues to give me strength.

—Cheryl

To my parents, Charles and Kathryn Roche, who inspired a love of learning and teaching.

—Emily

Uncovering Student Thinking
About **Mathematics**
in the **Common Core**

Grades K-2

20 Formative Assessment Probes

Cheryl Rose Tobey
Emily R. Fagan

CORWIN
A SAGE Company

FOR INFORMATION:

Corwin
A SAGE Company
2455 Teller Road
Thousand Oaks, California 91320
(800) 233-9936
www.corwin.com

SAGE Publications Ltd.
1 Oliver's Yard
55 City Road
London EC1Y 1SP
United Kingdom

SAGE Publications India Pvt. Ltd.
B 1/I 1 Mohan Cooperative Industrial Area
Mathura Road, New Delhi 110 044
India

SAGE Publications Asia-Pacific Pte. Ltd.
3 Church Street
#10-04 Samsung Hub
Singapore 049483

Acquisitions Editor: Jessica Allan
Associate Editor: Julie Nemer
Editorial Assistant: Heidi Arndt
Production Editors: Cassandra Margaret Seibel
       and Melanie Birdsall
Copy Editor: Cate Huisman
Typesetter: C&M Digitals (P) Ltd.
Proofreader: Victoria Reed-Castro
Indexer: Molly Hall
Cover Designer: Anupama Krishnan
Permissions Editor: Karen Ehrmann

Printed in the United States of America

Library of Congress Cataloging-in-Publication Data

Tobey, Cheryl Rose.

Uncovering student thinking about mathematics in the common core, grades K–2: 20 formative assessment probes/ Cheryl Rose Tobey, Emily R. Fagan.

pages cm
Includes bibliographical references and index.

ISBN 978-1-4522-3003-0 (pbk.)

1. Mathematics—Study and teaching (Early childhood)
2. Mathematical ability—Evaluation. 3. Individualized instruction. 4. Effective teaching. 5. Early childhood education. I. Fagan, Emily R. II. Title.

QA135.6.T59 2013
372.7'049—dc23   2013013375

This book is printed on acid-free paper.

13 14 15 16 17 10 9 8 7 6 5 4 3 2 1

Contents

Preface

Mathematics Assessment Probes

OVERVIEW

Formative assessment informs instruction and supports learning through a variety of methods and strategies aimed at determining students' prior knowledge of a learning target and using that information to drive instruction that supports each student in moving toward understanding of the learning target. Questioning, observation, and student self-assessment are examples of instructional strategies educators can incorporate to gain insight into student understanding. These instructional strategies become *formative assessment* if the results are used to plan and implement learning activities designed specifically to address the specific needs of the students.

This book focuses on using short sets of diagnostic questions, called *Mathematics Assessment Probes.* The Probes are designed to elicit prior understandings and commonly held misunderstandings and misconceptions. This elicitation allows the educator to make sound instructional choices targeted at a specific mathematics concept and responsive to the specific needs of a particular group of students.

> Diagnostic assessment is as important to teaching as a physical exam is to prescribing an appropriate medical regimen. At the outset of any unit of study, certain students are likely to have already mastered some of the skills that the teacher is about to introduce, and others may already understand key concepts. Some students are likely to be deficient in prerequisite skills or harbor misconceptions. Armed with this diagnostic information, a teacher gains greater insight into what to teach. (McTighe & O'Connor, 2005, p. 12)

The Mathematics Assessment Probes provided here are tools that enable grades K–2 school teachers to gather important insights in a practical way and that provide immediate information for planning purposes.

AUDIENCE

The first collection of Mathematics Assessment Probes and the accompanying Teacher Notes were written for the busy classroom teacher eager for thoughtful, research-based, diagnostic assessments focused on learning difficulties and aimed at enhancing the effectiveness of mathematics instruction. Since the publication of the first three *Uncovering Student Thinking in Mathematics Resources* books (Rose & Arline, 2009; Rose, Minton, & Arline, 2007; Rose Tobey & Minton, 2011), we have continually received requests for additional Probes. Both teachers and education leaders have communicated the need for a collection of research-based Probes that focus on a narrower grade span. In addition to additional Probes for each grade span, educators were eager for an alignment of the Probes to the Common Core Mathematics Standards (CCSSO, 2010). In response to these requests, we set to work writing, piloting, and field testing a more extensive set of Probes for primary teachers with a focus on targeting mathematics concepts within the new standards.

ORGANIZATION

This book is organized to provide readers with an understanding of the purpose, structure, and development of the Mathematics Assessment Probes as well as to support the use of applicable research and instructional strategies in mathematics classrooms.

Chapter 1 provides in-depth information about the process and design of the Mathematics Assessment Probes along with the development of an action-research structure we refer to as a QUEST cycle. Chapters 2 through 6 contain the collection of Probes categorized by concept strands with accompanying Teacher Notes to provide the specific research and instructional strategies for addressing students' challenges with mathematics. Chapter 7 highlights instructional considerations and images from practice to illuminate how easily and in how many varied ways the Probes can be used in mathematics classrooms. This chapter also highlights how use of the Probes can support students' proficiency with the Common Core's Mathematical Practices.

Acknowledgments

We would like to thank the many mathematics educators who during attendance at various professional development sessions gave valuable feedback about features of the Probes, including structures, concepts to target, and purposes of use.

We would especially like to acknowledge the contributions of the following educators who provided ideas and fieldtested Probes, gave feedback on Teacher Notes, scheduled classroom visits, and/or opened their classrooms to us to try Probes or interview students: Karla Bracy, Tracey Durham, Lynn Herdeman, Denise Inman, Catherine Judkins, Kelly Langbehn, Lauren LaPointe, Cathleen Maxfield, Candace Miller, Cynthia Powers, Nathan Merrill, Stephanie Pacanza, Kim Ramharter, Sarah Renz-Smith, Stephanie Rioux, Janet Shaw, Theresa Spisak, and Lisa Stevens.

A very special thanks to Laura Cummings, Laura Foley, and Susan Kane for their ongoing enthusiasm and implementation of the ideas from this book in their classrooms.

We would like to thank our Corwin editor, Jessica Allan, for her continued support and flexibility, and Page Keeley, our science colleague, who designed the process for developing diagnostic assessment Probes and who tirelessly promotes the use of these assessments for formative assessment purposes, helping to disseminate our work in her travels.

Mostly, we are grateful for the support, sacrifice, and patience shown by our families, Corey, Grandad, Carly, Jimmy, Bobby, Samantha, and Jack; and Sean, Nellie, and Seamus; throughout the writing this book.

PUBLISHER'S ACKNOWLEDGMENTS

Corwin gratefully acknowledges the contributions of the following reviewers:

Roxie R. Ahlbrecht, NBCT
Math Intervention Specialist
Lowell MST *IMAGINE, INNOVATE, INTERACT*
Sioux Falls, SD

About the Authors

 **Cheryl Rose Tobey** is a senior mathematics associate at Education Development Center (EDC) in Massachusetts. She is the project director for Formative Assessment in the Mathematics Classroom: Engaging Teachers and Students (FACETS) and a mathematics specialist for Differentiated Professional Development: Building Mathematics Knowledge for Teaching Struggling Students (DPD), both projects funded by the National Science Foundation (NSF). She also serves as a director of development for an Institute for Educational Science (IES) project, Eliciting Mathematics Misconceptions (EM2). Her work is primarily in the areas of formative assessment and professional development.

Prior to joining EDC, Tobey was the senior program director for mathematics at the Maine Mathematics and Science Alliance (MMSA), where she served as the co–principal investigator of the mathematics section of the NSF-funded Curriculum Topic Study, and principal investigator and project director of two Title IIa state Mathematics and Science Partnership projects. Prior to working on these projects, Tobey was the co–principal investigator and project director for MMSA's NSF-funded Local Systemic Change Initiative, Broadening Educational Access to Mathematics in Maine (BEAMM), and she was a fellow in Cohort 4 of the National Academy for Science and Mathematics Education Leadership. She is the coauthor of six published Corwin books, including three prior books in the *Uncovering Student Thinking* series (2007, 2009, 2011), two *Mathematics Curriculum Topic Study* resources (2006, 2012), and *Mathematics Formative Assessment: 75 Practical Strategies for Linking Assessment, Instruction and Learning* (2011). Before joining MMSA in 2001 to begin working with teachers, Tobey was a high school and middle school mathematics educator for 10 years. She received her BS in secondary mathematics education from the University of Maine at Farmington and her MEd from City University in Seattle. She currently lives in Maine with her husband and blended family of five children.

Emily R. Fagan is a senior curriculum design associate at Education Development Center (EDC) in Massachusetts. She has developed print and online curricula as well as professional development and assessment materials in mathematics for 12 years. She was project director of the MathScape Curriculum Center, a project funded by the National Science Foundation (NSF) to support schools, districts, and teachers in curriculum implementation, and she directed the revision of *MathScape: Seeing and Thinking Mathematically* (McGraw-Hill, 2005). She was a developer and facilitator in the Addressing Accessibility in Mathematics Project aimed at supporting struggling learners, particularly those with learning disabilities. Emily currently works on two NSF-funded projects: Differentiated Professional Development: Building Mathematics Knowledge for Teaching Struggling Students (DPD) and Formative Assessment in the Mathematics Classroom: Engaging Teachers and Students (FACETS).

Prior to joining EDC, Emily taught high school and middle school mathematics for nine years in Philadelphia and in Salem and Brookline, Massachusetts. She was a mentor teacher and member of the Massachusetts faculty of the Coalition of Essential Schools. She has long been interested in accessibility in mathematics education and improving opportunities for all students to learn and love math. While mathematics has been her focus for the last two decades, she has also taught science, social studies, and Spanish. Fagan holds an AB cum laude from Harvard University. She lives in Sudbury, Massachusetts, with her husband and two children.

1

Mathematics Assessment Probes

To differentiate instruction effectively, teachers need diagnostic assessment strategies to gauge their students' prior knowledge and uncover their misunderstandings. By accurately identifying and addressing areas of difficulties, teachers can help their students avoid becoming frustrated and disenchanted with mathematics and can prevent the perception that "some people just aren't good at math." Diagnostic strategies also support instruction that builds on individual students' existing understandings while addressing their identified difficulties. From infancy and through prekindergarten, children develop a base of skills, concepts, and misconceptions about numbers and mathematics (NRC, 2001, p. 157). Understanding and targeting these specific areas of difficulty enables teachers to perform focused and effective diagnostic assessment. The Mathematics Assessment Probes ("Probes") in this book allow teachers to target specific areas of difficulty as identified in research on student learning.

The Probes typically include a prompt or question and a series of responses designed specifically to elicit prior understandings and commonly held misunderstandings that may or may not be uncovered during an instructional unit. In the example in Figure 1.1, students are asked to choose from a selection of responses as well as write about how they determined their answer choice.

This combination of selected response and further explanation helps to guide teachers in making instructional choices based on the specific needs of students. Since not all Probes follow the same format, we will discuss the varying formats later in this chapter. If you are

Figure 1.1   Example of a Probe

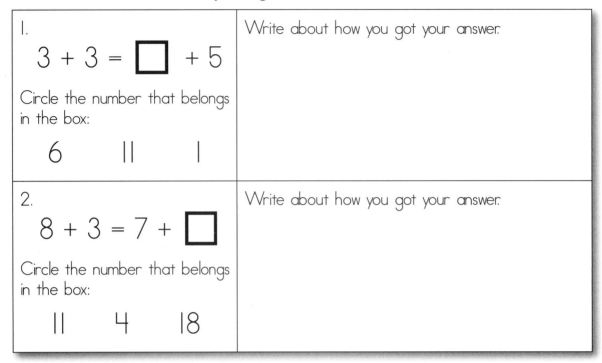

Completing Number Sentences

I. $3 + 3 = \square + 5$ Circle the number that belongs in the box: 6 II 1	Write about how you got your answer.
2. $8 + 3 = 7 + \square$ Circle the number that belongs in the box: II 4 I8	Write about how you got your answer.

wondering about what other kinds of Probes are included in this book, take a few moments to review two or three additional Probes from Chapters 2–6 before continuing reading, but we strongly suggest that you return to read the rest of this chapter before beginning to use the Probes with your students.

Are you wondering about the Probes? If you are, we suggest reviewing the following Probes as initial examples:

- Name the Missing Number Interview Probe p. 38
- Is it a Triangle? Probe Sort p. 148
- Are They Equivalent? Probe p. 92

Are you wondering about the Probes? If you are, we suggest reviewing the following Probes as initial examples:

- Name the Missing Number Interview Probe p. 38
- Is It a Triangle? Probe Sort p. 148
- Are They Equivalent? Probe p. 92

At this point, you may be asking; "What is the difference between Mathematics Assessment Probes and other assessments?" Comprehensive diagnostic assessments for primary grade mathematics such as Key Math3 (Pearson) and assessments from the Northwest Education Association (NWEA) as well as the many state- and district-developed assessments can provide information important for finding entry points and current levels of understanding within a defined progression of learning for a particular mathematics subdomain such as counting and cardinality. Such assessments will continue to play an important role in schools, as they allow teachers to get a snapshot of student understanding across multiple subdomains, often at intervals throughout the year depending on the structure of the assessment.

How are Probes different? Consider the following vignette:

> In a primary classroom, students are having a "math talk" to decide which figures are triangles. After using a card sort strategy to individually group picture cards as "triangles" and "not triangles," the teacher encourages the students to develop a list of characteristics that could be used to decide whether a figure is a triangle. As students share their ideas and come to an agreement, the teacher records the characteristic and draws an example and nonexample to further illustrate the idea. She then gives students an opportunity to regroup their cards, using the defining characteristics they have developed as a class. As the students discuss the results of their sorting process, she listens for and encourages students to use the listed characteristics to justify their choices. Throughout the discussion, the class works together to revise the triangle characteristics already listed and to add additional characteristics that were not included in the initial discussion (excerpt from Keeley & Rose Tobey, 2011, p. 1).

The Probe in this vignette, the *Triangle Card Sort,* serves as a diagnostic assessment at several points during the lesson. The individual elicitation allows the teacher to diagnose students' current understanding; the conversation about characteristics both builds the teacher's understanding of what students are thinking and creates a learning experience for students to further develop their understanding of the characteristics of triangles. The individual time allotted for regrouping the cards allows the teacher to assess whether students are able to integrate this new knowledge with former conceptions or whether additional instruction or intervention is necessary.

Rather than addressing a variety of math concepts, Probes focus on a particular subconcept within a larger mathematical idea. By pinpointing one subconcept, the assessment can be embedded at the lesson level to address conceptions and misconceptions while learning is underway, helping to bridge from diagnostic to formative assessment.

Helping all students build understanding in mathematics is an important and challenging goal. Being aware of student difficulties and the sources of those difficulties, and designing instruction to diminish them, are important steps in achieving this goal (Yetkin, 2003). The process of using a Probe to diagnose student understandings and misunderstandings and then responding with instructional decisions based on the new information is the key to helping students build their mathematical knowledge. Let's take a look at the complete Probe implementation process we call the *QUEST Cycle* (Figure 1.2).

Figure 1.2 Quest Cycle

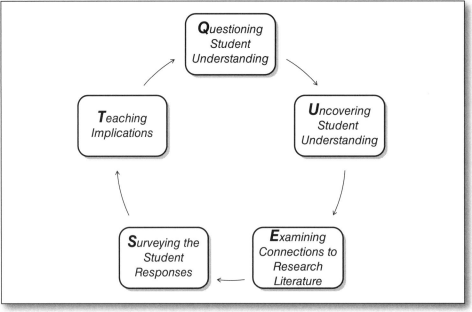

Source: Adapted from Rose, Minton, & Arline (2007).

- **Q**uestioning student understanding: Determine the key mathematical understandings you want students to learn.
- **U**ncovering student understanding: Use a Probe to uncover understandings and areas of difficulties.
- **E**xamining connections to research and educational literature: Prepare to answer the question: In what ways do your students' understandings relate to those described in the research base?
- **S**urveying the student responses: Analyze student responses to better understand the various levels of understanding demonstrated in their work.
- **T**eaching implications: Consider and follow through with next steps to move student learning forward.

Note that in the *Triangle Sort Vignette,* this cycle is repeated several times within the described instructional period.

The remaining parts of this chapter describe important components of the QUEST Cycle for implementing Probes, including background information on the key mathematics, the structure of the Probes, and connections to the research base. In addition, you will learn about how to get started with administering the Probes.

QUESTIONING STUDENT UNDERSTANDING: DETERMINE THE KEY MATHEMATICAL CONCEPTS YOU WANT STUDENTS TO LEARN

The Common Core State Standards for Mathematics (referred to as the Common Core) define what students should understand and are the basis for the targeted mathematics concepts addressed by the Probes in this book. These understandings include both conceptual and procedural knowledge, both of which are important for students' mathematical development.

> Research has strongly established that proficiency in subjects such as mathematics requires conceptual understanding. When students understand mathematics, they are able to use their knowledge flexibly. They combine factual knowledge, procedural facility, and conceptual understanding in powerful ways. (NCTM, 2000, p. 20)

Think about the experience of following step-by-step driving directions to an unfamiliar destination using the commands of a GPS but never having viewed a road map of the area. Although it may be easy to follow the directions one step at a time, if you lose your satellite reception, you will likely not know where to turn next or even which direction to head. Using a GPS without a road map is like learning procedures in math without understanding the concepts behind those procedures. Learners who

Table 1.1 Procedural Versus Conceptual Understanding

Factual Knowledge: Procedures, Skills, and Facts	Accompanying Conceptual Understanding	Examples
Learn and apply a series of steps	• Explain why the steps make sense mathematically • Use reasoning to rebuild the steps if needed • Make connections between alternate steps that also can be used to find the solution	When adding 23 and 12, can describe and connect two different methods for adding these two-digit numbers Can interpret a graph to tell about a data set
Find the answer	• Justify whether the answer makes sense (numerical example: reasoning about the size of numbers and a mathematical operation) • Troubleshoot a mistake • Represent thinking with symbols, models, and/or diagrams • Show flexibility in representing mathematical situations	Can reason that 13 + 15 must be between 20 and 30, since there are only two tens plus some ones Can sort a collection of geometric shapes in more than one way by attending to their attributes
Memorize facts	• Generate answer quickly when unable to recall a fact (automaticity)	Has an efficient method to add facts not remembered by recall: 6 + 9 (add 10; go back 1) 3 + 4 (doubles plus 1) 3 + 8 (make a 10 with 2 and 8; add 1 more)

follow the steps of a mathematical procedure, without any conceptual understanding connected to that procedure, may get lost when they make a mistake. Understanding the bigger picture enables learners to reason about a solution and/or reconstruct a procedure.

This relationship between understanding concepts and being proficient with procedures is complex. Table 1.1 provides some examples of each type of understanding for a variety of contexts.

The relationship between understanding concepts and being proficient with procedures is further developed in the examples of the Probes that follow. Both conceptual understanding and procedural flexibility are important goals that complement each other in developing strong mathematical abilities. Each is necessary, and only together do they become sufficient. The examples of Probes in Figures 1.3, 1.4, and 1.5 will further distinguish conceptual and procedural understandings.

Example 1: Chicken and Eggs Probe

In the Chicken and Eggs Probe, students with conceptual and procedural understanding pay attention to the *number* of objects rather than other characteristics, including size and arrangement. The task moves students beyond just counting by asking them to compare "how many" and elicits conceptual understanding of cardinality. The task can also elicit flexibility in determining how to count a set of objects (rote counting versus one-to-one counting versus cardinality). More information about this Probe can be found on pages 29–37.

Example 2: Length of Rope Probe

In the Length of Rope Probe, students with conceptual and procedural understanding pay attention to how the unit (the minicrayon) has been tiled. Students who have conceptual understanding look for repeated tiling of the unit without gaps or overlap and can determine when additional units are needed to determine a length. They understand length measure as more than just where the end of an object aligns to the number of tiled units and that the orientation of the unit matters only when it impacts the unit's length. More information about this Probe can be found on pages 128–134.

Example 3: Solving Number Stories Probe

In the Solving Number Stories Probe, students with conceptual and procedural understanding pay attention to the context of the problems to determine whether the numbers should be joined, separated, or compared. Rather than focusing solely on key words as a problem-solving approach, these students are able to represent the problem based on an approach that models the situation. Students can solve the problem accurately and can describe how the numbers involved in modeling the problem relate back to the context. More information about this Probe can be found on pages 121–125.

Figure 1.3 Chicken and Eggs Problems 1 and 2

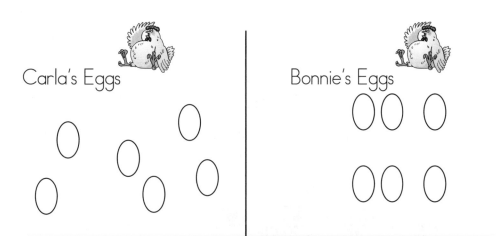

Carla's Eggs

Bonnie's Eggs

Who has more eggs? Circle the letter.

A. Carla has more eggs.   B. Bonnie has more eggs.

C. Carla and Bonnie have the same number of eggs.

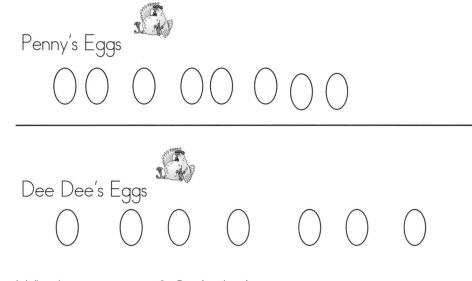

Penny's Eggs

Dee Dee's Eggs

Who has more eggs? Circle the letter.

A. Penny has more eggs.   B. Dee Dee has more eggs.

C. Penny and Dee Dee have the same number of eggs.

Figure 1.4   Length of Rope

Length of Rope

Susie is using minicrayons to measure different-size pieces of rope. The pieces of rope and minicrayons are shown below.

Problems 1–3

Decide if each piece of Susie's rope is 3 minicrayons long.	Circle One
1	 Yes No
2	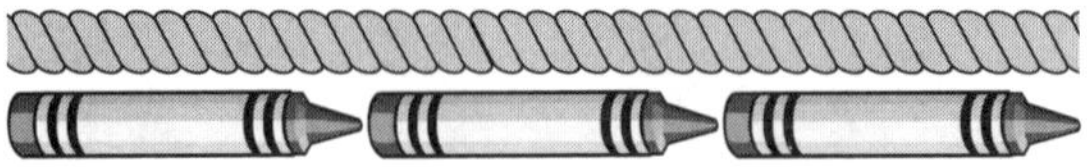 Yes No
3	 Yes No

Explain how you decided whether to circle Yes or No:

Problems 4–6

Decide if each piece of Susie's rope is 3 minicrayons long.	Circle One
4	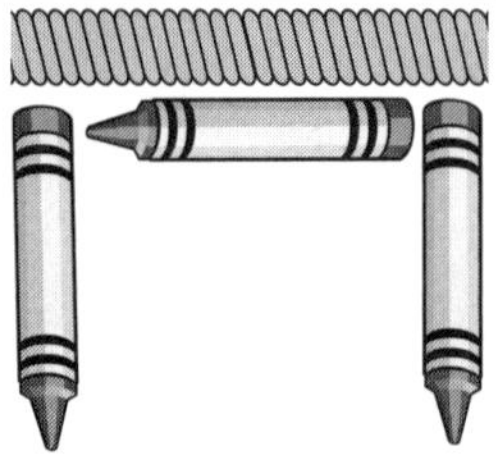 Yes No
5	 Yes No
6	 Yes No

Explain how you decided whether to circle Yes or No:

Figure 1.5 Solving Number Stories

1. Three students each solved the following problem.

Mike has 23 toy cars. Susan has 31 toy cars. How many more toy cars does Susan have than Mike?

I think the answer is 54 — Lamar

I think the answer is 8 — Fran

I don't think the answer is 54 or 8 — Tom

Circle the name of the student you agree with. Use words or pictures to show your thinking.

2. Three students each solved the following problem.

Paula has some grapes. Carlos gave her 18 more grapes. Now Paula has 34 grapes. How many grapes did Paula have to start with?

I think the answer is 52 — Stefan

I think the answer is 16 — Tasha

I don't think the answer is 52 or 16 — Emma

Circle the name of the student you agree with. Use words or pictures to show your thinking.

UNCOVERING STUDENT UNDERSTANDING: USE A PROBE TO UNCOVER UNDERSTANDINGS AND AREAS OF DIFFICULTIES

Misunderstandings are likely to develop as a normal part of learning mathematics. These misunderstandings can be classified as conceptual misunderstandings, overgeneralizations, preconceptions, and partial conceptions. These are summarized in Figure 1.6, and each is described in more detail below.

In *Hispanic and Anglo Students' Misconceptions in Mathematics*, Jose Mestre (1989) summarized cognitive research as follows: Students do not come to the classroom as "blank slates" (Resnick, 1983). Instead, they come with theories constructed from their everyday experiences. They have actively constructed these theories, an activity crucial to all successful learning. Some of the theories that students use to make sense of the world are, however, incomplete half-truths (Mestre, 1987). They are misconceptions.

Misconceptions are a problem for two reasons. First, when students use them to interpret new experiences, misconceptions interfere with learning. Second, because they have actively constructed them, students are emotionally and intellectually attached to their misconceptions. Even when students recognize that their misconceptions can harm their learning, they are reluctant to let them go. Given this, it is critical that primary teachers uncover and address their students' misconceptions as early as possible.

For the purposes of this book, misconceptions will be categorized as *overgeneralizations, preconceptions, partial conceptions,* and *conceptual*

Figure 1.6 Mathematics Assessment Probes

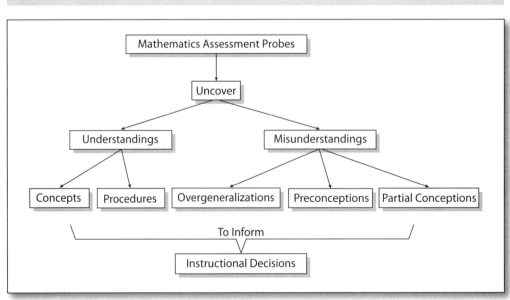

Source: Adapted from Rose, Minton, & Arline (2007).

misunderstandings. The following brief summary describes each of these categories of misconception.

- **Preconceptions:** Ideas students have developed from previous experiences, including everyday interactions and school experiences. Often preconceptions are accurate at the level of mathematics experience but could be an issue if students do not consciously integrate new mathematical ideas.
- **Overgeneralizations:** Information extended or applied to another context in an inappropriate way. This also includes vernacular issues related to differences between the everyday meanings of words and their mathematical meanings.
- **Partial Conceptions:** Hybrids of correct and incorrect ideas. This may result from difficulty generalizing or connecting concepts or distinguishing between two concepts.
- **Conceptual Misunderstandings:** Content students "learned" in school but have misinterpreted and internalized and that often goes unnoticed by the teacher. Students often make their own meaning out of what is taught. (Above categories adapted from Keeley, 2012)

Table 1.2 provides an example from each of the above categories. The examples provided are from progressions for the Common Core State Standards in Mathematics written by the Common Core Standards Writing Team (2011a, 2011b).

Some misunderstandings do not fall distinctly into one category but can be characterized in more than one way. For example, the conceptual misunderstanding of the equal sign as "the answer is" can also be considered an overgeneralization. In addition, some misconceptions are more deeply rooted and difficult to change than others. It is important to make the distinction between what we might call a silly mistake and a more fundamental one, which may be the product of a deep-rooted misunderstanding. In her guest editorial titled "Misunderstanding Misconceptions," Page Keeley described various practitioner misunderstandings related to using the Science Probes in the National Science Teachers Association's *Uncovering Student Ideas in Science* series (Keeley, 2012). Both in our work with Page and with mathematics educators using the *Uncovering Student Thinking in Mathematics* resources, we have encountered many similar misunderstandings among teachers:

- *All misconceptions are the same.* The word *misconception* is frequently used to describe all ideas students bring to their learning that are not completely accurate. In contrast, researchers often use labels such as *alternative frameworks, naïve ideas, phenomenological primitives, children's ideas,* et cetera, to imply that these ideas are not completely "wrong" in a student's common-sense world.
- *Misconceptions are a bad thing.* The word *misconception* seems to have a pejorative connotation to most practitioners. According to constructivist theory, when new ideas are encountered, they are either accepted, rejected, or modified to fit existing conceptions. It is the

Table 1.2 Misconceptions: Categories and Examples

Misconception Category	Example
Preconceptions: Ideas students have from previous experiences, including everyday interactions	• Students usually know or can learn to say the counting words up to a given number before they can use these numbers to count objects or to tell the number of objects. Students become fluent in saying the count sequence so that they have enough attention to focus on the pairings involved in counting objects (p. 4).
Overgeneralizations: Extending information to another context in an inappropriate way	• When counting two sets of objects, students learn that even if one group looks as if it has more objects (e.g., has some extra sticking out), matching or counting may reveal a different result (p. 5). • The language of comparisons can be difficult. For example, "Julie has three more apples than Lucy" tells both that Julie has more apples and that the difference is three. Many students "hear" the part of the sentence about who has more, but do not initially hear the part about how many more. Another language issue is that the comparing sentence might be stated in either of two related ways, using "more" or "less" (p. 12).
Partial Conceptions: Using some correct and some incorrect ideas. This may result from difficulty generalizing or connecting concepts or distinguishing between two concepts.	• Students understand that the last number name said in counting tells the number of objects counted. Prior to reaching this understanding, a student who is asked "How many kittens?" may regard the counting performance itself as the answer, instead of answering with the cardinality of the set (p. 4). • The make-a-ten methods are more difficult in English than in East Asian languages because of the irregularities and reversals in the teen number words (p. 16).
Conceptual Misunderstandings: Content that students "learn" in school but have misinterpreted and internalized and that often goes unnoticed by the teacher. Students often make their own meaning out of what is taught.	• Equations with one number on the left and an operation on the right (e.g., $5 = 2 + 3$ to record a group of 5 things decomposed as a group of 2 things and a group of 3 things) allow students to understand equations as showing in various ways that the quantities on both sides have the same value (p. 10). Students who only see equations written in one way often misunderstand the meaning of the equal sign and think that the "answer" always needs to be to the right of the equal sign.

cognitive dissonance students experience when they realize an existing mental model no longer works for them that makes students willing to give up a preexisting idea in favor of a scientific one. Having ideas to work from, even if they are not completely accurate, leads to deeper understanding when students engage in a conceptual-change process (Watson & Konicek, 1990).

- *All misconceptions are major barriers to learning.* Just as some learning standards have more weight in promoting conceptual learning than others, the same is true of misconceptions. For example, a student may have a misconception for only one type of problem situation (see Figure 1.5, Solving Number Stories) but can make great strides in learning to model and represent operations for other situations (adapted from Keeley, 2012).

To teach in a way that avoids creating any misconceptions is not possible, and we have to accept that students will make some incorrect generalizations that will remain hidden unless the teacher makes specific efforts to uncover them (Askew & Wiliam, 1995). Our job as educators is to minimize the chances of students' harboring misconceptions by knowing the potential difficulties students are likely to encounter, using assessments to elicit misconceptions and implementing instruction designed to build new and accurate mathematical ideas.

The primary purpose of the Probes is to elicit understandings and areas of difficulties related to specific mathematics ideas. In addition to these content-specific targets, the Probes also elicit skills and processes related to the Standards for Mathematical Practices, especially those related to use of reasoning and explanation. If you are unfamiliar with the Standards for Mathematical Practices, descriptions of them can be found in Appendix A.

WHAT IS THE STRUCTURE OF A PROBE?

Each Probe is designed to include two levels of response, one for elicitation of common understandings and misunderstandings and the other for the elaboration of individual student thinking. Each of the levels is described in more detail below.

Level 1: Answer Response

Since the elicitation level is designed to uncover common understandings and misunderstandings, a structured format using stems, correct answers, and distractors is used to narrow ideas found in the related research. The formats typically fall into one of four categories, shown in Figures 1.7 through 1.10.

Selected Response

- Two or more items are provided, each with one stem, one correct answer, and one or more distractors.

Math Talk Probe

- Two or more statements are provided, and students choose the statement they agree with. This format is adapted from *Concept Cartoons in Science Education*, created by Stuart Naylor and Brenda Keogh (2000) for probing student ideas in science.

Figure 1.7 Chicken and Eggs Multiple Selections Probe Problems 3 and 4

Nina's Eggs

Nellie's Eggs

Who has more eggs? Circle the letter.
A. Nina has more eggs.   B. Nellie has more eggs.
C. Nina and Nellie have the same number of eggs.

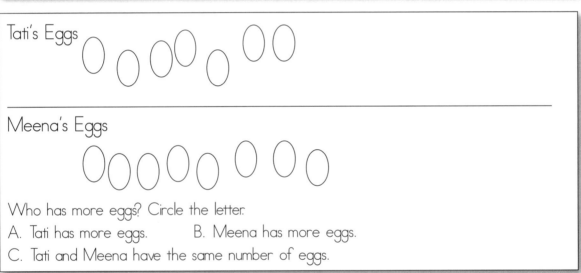

Tati's Eggs

Meena's Eggs

Who has more eggs? Circle the letter.
A. Tati has more eggs.   B. Meena has more eggs.
C. Tati and Meena have the same number of eggs.

Examples and Nonexamples Card Sort

- Several examples and nonexamples are given, and students are asked to sort the items into the correct piles.

Justified List

- Two or more separate problems or statements are provided, and students must justify each answer they choose as correct.

Level 2: Explanation of Response Choice

The second level of each of the Probes is designed so students can elaborate on the reasoning they used to respond to the Level 1 elicitation question. Mathematics teachers gain a wealth of information by delving into the

Figure 1.8 Comparing Measures Math Talk Probe

Comparing Measures

Two students were asked to measure the length of a book using either an eraser or a paperclip. The picture shows how these items compare in size.

Kyra and Toby both measured the same book using one of the items from the picture above.

Kyra   Toby

If both of them are correct, what items did they measure with?

	Circle One	
Kyra:	eraser	paperclip
	Circle One	
Toby:	eraser	paperclip

Explain your choices.

thinking behind students' answers, not just when answers are wrong but also when they are correct (Burns, 2005). Although the Level 1 answers and distractors are designed to target common understandings and misunderstandings, the elaboration level allows educators to look more deeply at student thinking. Often a student chooses a specific response, correct or incorrect, for a typical reason. Also, there are many different ways to approach a problem correctly; therefore, the elaboration level allows educators to look for trends in thinking and in methods used. At the early grades, much of this elaboration is done through verbal exchanges with students while administering the Probe, shifting to written elaborations as students develop the ability to write them. Chapter 7 delves deeper into expectations for this elaboration and its relationship to the Common Core Mathematical Practices.

Figure 1.9 Is It a Triangle? Examples and Nonexamples Card Sort

Advance Preparation: Create cards by photocopying on card stock and cutting. Separate the two blank cards and the two label cards from the deck, and shuffle the rest of the cards.

Instructions:

1. Invite the student(s) to sort the cards into two piles: Triangle and NOT a Triangle. Use the label cards to identify the piles.

2. As students finish the sort, give them the blank cards, and ask them to create their own Triangle and NOT a Triangle cards.

3. Ask students to choose three cards from the Triangle pile (or choose three cards for them). Ask them to explain or show how they knew these cards should go in the Triangle pile.

4. Ask students to choose three cards from the NOT a Triangle pile (or choose three cards for them). Ask them to explain or show how they knew these cards should go in the NOT a Triangle pile. Use the recording sheet as appropriate.

QUEST CYCLE: STRUCTURE OF THE SUPPORTING TEACHER NOTES

The Teacher Notes, included with each Probe, have been designed to help you prepare for a QUEST Cycle. The first two components of the cycle, *determining questions around the key mathematics* and *uncovering student understandings and areas of difficulties*, have been described more fully above. We will use the description of the Teacher Notes to provide more details about the remaining components of the cycle.

Questions to Consider About the Key Mathematical Concepts

This section of the Teacher Notes helps to focus a teacher on the key conceptual and procedural mathematics addressed by the particular Probe and gives information about alignment to Common Core standards at a particular grade level. Figure 1.11 shows an example from this section of the Chicken and Eggs Probe Teacher Notes.

Figure 1.10 Are They Equivalent?

1. Without adding the two numbers, use what you know about adding three-digit numbers to decide which of the number expressions below are equivalent to

427 + 569

	Circle One	Explain Your Answer
A. 724 + 965	Yes No	
B. 467 + 529	Yes No	
C. 527 + 469	Yes No	
D. 472 + 596	Yes No	
E. 927 + 69	Yes No	

2. Without subtracting, use what you know about subtracting three-digit numbers to decide which of the number expressions below are equivalent to

618 – 498

	Circle One	Explain Your Answer
A. 620 – 500	Yes No	
B. 681 – 489	Yes No	
C. 608 – 488	Yes No	
D. 698 – 418	Yes No	
E. 618 – 418 – 80	Yes No	

Figure 1.11 Questions to Consider About the Key Mathematical Concepts

Do students apply counting and cardinality when comparing two sets of objects? To what extent do they

- apply rote counting along with an understanding of one-to-one correspondence when they match one object in the set to one count?
- continue through a sequence of counting numbers, "1, 2, 3, 4," and so on until they've counted the whole set?
- answer the question "how many are there?" with the last number they have counted?

Common Core Connection (K.CC)

Grade: Kindergarten

Domain: Counting and Cardinality (CC)

Clusters:

B. Count to tell the number of objects.

K.CC.B.4. Understand the relationship between numbers and quantities; connect counting to cardinality.

K.CC.B.5. Count to answer "how many?" questions about as many as 20 things arranged in a line, a rectangular array, or a circle, or as many as 10 things in a scattered configuration; given a number from 1–20, count out that many objects.

C. Compare numbers.

K.CC.C.6. Identify whether the number of objects in one group is greater than, less than, or equal to the number of objects in another group, e.g., by using matching and counting strategies.

Uncovering Student Understanding About the Key Concepts

This section of the Teacher Notes (Figure 1.12) breaks down the concepts and ideas described in the "Questioning" section into specific understandings and areas of difficulty targeted by the Probe.

Exploring Excerpts From Educational Resources and Related Research

This section of the Teacher Notes (Figure 1.13) includes excerpts from cognitive research related to the common areas of difficulty targeted by the Probe. The excerpts are meant to provide some background from the research base behind the development of the Probe. The references provide an opportunity for you to seek additional information when needed.

This research base is an important component in the Probe development process. More information on the origin of the Probe development process can be found in Appendix B.

Figure 1.12 Uncovering Student Understanding About the Key Concepts

Using the Chicken and Eggs Probe can provide the following information about how the students are thinking about counting and cardinality.

Do they

- recognize that the arrangement of a group of objects does not change the count?

- give the last number they've counted as the count of the set of objects?

- apply one-to-one correspondence, applying just one counting number to each object they count?

- understand how to use the count of two sets to compare them, using words such as *more* or *less*?

OR

OR

OR

OR

Do they

- think that the arrangement of the eggs determines which is greater?

- begin to count all over again when asked how many there are?

- skip over eggs when they are counting, or double-count eggs?

- compare the size of the eggs or how they are spaced or arranged rather than the quantities?

Figure 1.13 Exploring Excerpts From Educational Resources and Related Research

Common areas of difficulty for students:

"Counting one past the actual number of items—Young children often have difficulty tagging items (touching and saying a number) and partitioning (moving aside counted items) simultaneously. This often leads to saying one extra number name." (Bay Area Mathematics Task Force, 1999, p. 10)

Misusing the acoustical sequence of numbers. Instead of counting per word (numeral), they count per syllable. For example, sev-en means 2 objects; e-lev-en means 3 objects. (Van Den Brink, 1984, p. 2)

Thinking sets of objects that are spread out have a larger count than those that are arranged close to one another. Students are "misled by perceptual clues—six items spread out may appear to be more than 7 items close together." (Bay Area Mathematics Task Force, 1999, p. 10)

When a student can count 4 objects (1, 2, 3, 4) and can answer "4" when asked "How many are there?" the student has developed cardinality. Children who understand the short cut to describing the count of a set by using the last number of the enumeration of the count (4) rather than repeating the whole count (1, 2, 3, 4) are said to have grasped the *cardinality principle.* (Gelman & Gallistel, 1978; Schaeffer, Eggleston, & Scott, 1974)

Surveying the Prompts and Selected Responses in the Probe

This section of the Teacher Notes (Figure 1.14) includes information about the prompt, selected response/answer(s), and the distractors. Sample student responses are given for a selected number of elicited understandings and misunderstandings. This initial preparation will help expedite the analysis process once you administer the Probe to students.

Figure 1.14 Surveying the Prompts and Selected Responses in the Probe

There are four cards, each containing two sets of objects to compare. The items are designed to elicit understandings and common difficulties as described below.

Carla and Bonnie

If a student chooses	It is likely that the student
Carla has more eggs	• thinks that the arrangement of a set of objects is related to the size or count of the set of objects (more spread out or random is larger).
Bonnie has more eggs	• counts incorrectly or has difficulty with comparison words like *same* or *more*.
Carla and Bonnie have the same number of eggs (correct answer)	• applies one-to-one correspondence and other counting strategies and is able to compare quantities using *same* and *more*.

Penny and Dee Dee

If a student chooses	It is likely that the student
Penny has more eggs	• is applying accurate counting and comparison strategies.
Dee Dee has more eggs	• has a misconception that objects that are spread out in an arrangement are "more" than objects arranged more closely to one another. (See Sample Student Response 1, Figure 1.16.)
Penny and Dee Dee have the same number of eggs	• has made a counting error, such as missing or double-counting an egg.

Teaching Implications and Considerations

Being aware of student difficulties and their sources is important, but acting on that information to design and provide instruction that will diminish those difficulties is even more important. The information in this section of the Teacher Notes (Figure 1.15) is broken into two categories: (1) ideas for eliciting more information from students about their understanding and difficulties, and (2) ideas for planning instruction in response to what you learned from the results of administering the Probe. Although these ideas are included in the Teacher Notes, we strongly encourage you to pursue additional research-based teaching implications.

Figure 1.15 Teaching Implications and Considerations

Ideas for eliciting more information from students about their understanding and difficulties:

- How can you tell that _____ has more eggs than _____?
- Does it matter which egg you start with when you count?
- Is there more than one way to determine who has more eggs?
- What happens when some eggs are bigger than other eggs? (Refer to Nina and Nellie or Tati and Mina card.)
- How do you count the eggs when they are in a line? In rows? In a mixed up jumble? (Refer to Carla and Bonnie and Penny and Dee Dee cards.)

Ideas for planning instruction in response to what you learned from the results of administering the probe:

- Use concrete materials. Skill in counting is supported by providing sets of blocks or counters that students can manipulate as they are counting. These concrete materials can help to build understanding of one-to-one correspondence and provide engaging practice in matching number names with the objects being counted. Counting objects arranged in one straight row is easier for children than counting objects arranged randomly or in organized rectangular array or circles.
- Provide opportunities for students to build or draw sets of different sizes to build understanding of comparative terminology. Ask students to create two groups of counters, one that is more than the other. Give students practice building sets that fit certain criteria for comparison: the same, more, or less.
- Be explicit about counting guidelines—each object must be counted once and only once—and discuss strategies for counting. How do you keep track of items you have already counted? Does it matter where you start when you are counting a set? How do you decide where to start? Do you use any shortcuts when you are counting a set of objects?
- Write numbers to show the counts of sets of objects: Students need experiences in connecting the number name with its numeral representation. Connecting the last number counted with its numeric representation can support the idea of cardinality—I count up until I've counted each object, and the last name I count is the number of objects. I can describe the count by saying or writing a number.

Included in the Teaching section of the Teacher Notes are sample student responses; examples of these are shown in Figure 1.16.

Figure 1.16   Sample Student Responses to Chicken and Eggs Probe

Responses That Suggest Difficulty

Sample Student Response 1

Student: Dee Dee has more eggs than Penny.

Teacher: How do you know?

Student: Dee Dee's eggs go all the way to here (points to the last egg on the right) and Penny's go to here (points to the last egg on the right).

Teacher: How many eggs does Dee Dee have?

Student: 7

Teacher: And how many eggs does Penny have?

Student: 8

Teacher: And Dee Dee has more eggs.

Student: Yes.

Sample Student Response 2

Student: Nina has more eggs.

Teacher: Nina has more eggs than Nellie?

Student: Yes.

Teacher: How do you know?

Student: The eggs are bigger?

Teacher: Yes, the eggs are bigger. Are there more eggs here (pointing to Nina's eggs) than here (pointing to Nellie's eggs)?

Student: Yes.

Responses That Suggest Understanding

Sample Student Response 3

Student: (Pointing to Tati's eggs and counting) 1, 2, 3, 4, 5, 6, 7. 7 eggs. (Pointing to Meena's eggs and counting) 1, 2, 3, 4, 5, 6, 7, 8. 8 eggs.

Teacher: Does Tati have more eggs? Does Meena have more eggs? Or do they have the same number of eggs?

Student: Meena has more eggs.

Teacher: Why do you say Meena has more eggs?

Student: She has 8 eggs, and 8 is 1 more than 7.

Figure 1.17   Reflection Template

Questions to Consider About the Key Mathematical Concepts

What is the concept you wish to target? Is the concept at grade level, or is it a prerequisite?

Uncovering Student Understanding About the Key Concepts

How will you collect information from students (e.g., paper and pencil, interview, student response system, etc.)? What form will you use (e.g., one-page Probe, card sort, etc.)? Are there adaptations you plan to make? Review the summary of typical student responses.

Exploring Excerpts From Educational Resources and Related Research

Review the quotes from research about common difficulties related to the Probe. What do you predict to be common understandings and/or misunderstandings for your students?

Surveying the Prompts and Selected Responses in the Probe

Sort by selected responses; then re-sort by patterns in thinking. What common understandings/misunderstandings did the Probe elicit? How do these elicited understanding/ misunderstandings compare to those listed in the Teacher Notes?

Teaching Implications and Considerations

Review the bulleted list, and decide how you will take action. What actions did you take? How did you assess the impact of those actions? What are your next steps?

Variations

For some Probes, adaptations and variations are provided and can be found following the Teacher Notes and sample student responses to the Probe. A variation of a Probe provides an alternate structure (selected response, multiple selections, opposing views, or examples/nonexamples) for the question within the same grade span. In contrast, an adaptation to a Probe is similar in content to the original, but the level of mathematics is changed for a different grade span.

Action Research Reflection Template

A reflection template is included in Appendix C. The reflection template provides a structured approach to working through the QUEST cycle with a Probe. The components of the template are described in Figure 1.17.

BEGINNING TO USE THE PROBES

Now that you have a background on the design of the Probes, the accompanying Teacher Notes, and the QUEST Cycle, it is time to think about how to get started using the Probes with your students.

Choosing a Probe: Determining which Probe to use depends on a number of factors, including time of year, alignment to curriculum, and range of abilities within your classroom. We recommend you spend some time reviewing the Probes at your grade level first but also make note of additional Probes that may be appropriate for your students.

Deciding how to administer a Probe: Depending on your purpose, Probes can be given to one student or to all students in your classroom. You may wish to give a Probe to only one student (or several) if you notice the student or group is struggling with a related concept. By giving a Probe to all students, you can gain a sense of patterns of understanding and difficulty in order to target instruction. All Probes can be given as verbal interviews, and many of the kindergarten Probes are written as verbal interviews, but we encourage you whenever appropriate to ask students to write and/or draw their responses instead of explaining them verbally. Many teachers script above what the students have written, a practice that students may already be familiar with from their writing instruction. Scripting is a handwritten record of the student's spoken explanation and the teacher's related notes. Chapter 7 includes additional instructional considerations.

Talking with students about Probes: We have found that young students are very much able to understand the diagnostic nature of the Probes, especially if the process is shared explicitly with them. Talk to your students about the importance of explaining their thinking in mathematics and why you will ask additional questions to understand more about their thinking.

When giving a Probe, be sure to read through the directions, repeating them as necessary. Do not try to correct students on the spot; instead, ask additional probing questions to determine whether the additional questions prompt the student to think differently. If not, do not stop to try to teach the students "in the moment." Instead, take in the information and think about the next appropriate instructional steps. If students are having difficulty, reassure them that you will be working with them to learn more about the content in the Probe.

HOW TO NAVIGATE THE BOOK

This chapter provided the background information needed to begin to dig into the Probes and think about how you will use them with your students. The next five chapters include 20 sets of Probes and accompanying Teacher Notes, and the final chapter includes additional considerations for using the Probes.

Chapters 2 Through 6: The Probes

Many of the mathematics assessment Probes included in this book fall under the topic of number and operations, because the cognitive research is abundant in these areas (Clements & Sarama, 2004), and the Common Core places a strong emphasis on number and operation concepts at grades K–2. Figure 1.18 provides an "at a glance" look at the targeted grade span and related domain of the content of the Probes.

The beginning of each Probe chapter (Chapters 2–6) includes background on the development of the Probes to align with the relevant Common Core domain and standards and a summary chart to guide your review and selection of Probes and variations to use with your students.

Chapters 7: Additional Considerations

The QUEST Cycle components are explained in detail within this chapter as well as for each specific Probe through the accompanying Teacher Notes. In addition to these "specific to the Probe" ideas are instructional considerations that cut across the Probes. Such considerations include ways to use the Probes over time to promote mathematical discussions, support and assess students' ability to provide justification, and promote conceptual change.

We recommend that you scan the contents of Chapter 7 before beginning to use the Probes but that you not to try to "do it all" the first time out. After experiencing the use of the Probes, return to Chapter 7 to pinpoint one or two considerations to implement.

FINAL CHAPTER 1 THOUGHTS

We hope these Probes will support you in your work in trying to uncover your students' thinking and understanding and will inspire you to explore ways to respond to their strengths and difficulties in order to support students in moving their learning forward.

Figure 1.18 Mathematics Assessment Probes

		Kindergarten	
Chapter	Page Numbers	Probe	CCSS Domain
2	p. 29	Chicken and Eggs	Counting and Cardinality
2	p. 38	Name the Missing Number	Counting and Cardinality
2	p. 46	Dots and Numerals: Card Match	Counting and Cardinality
2	p. 54	Counting and Combining	Counting and Cardinality
2	p. 61	Comparing Numbers	Number and Operations in Base Ten
6	p. 150	Is It a Triangle?	Geometry
6	p. 159	Is It Two Dimensional or Three Dimensional?	Geometry
		Grade 1	
3	p. 69	What's the Value of the Digit?	Number and Operations in Base Ten
4	p. 103	Apples and Oranges	Operations and Algebraic Thinking
4	p. 109	Sums of Ten	Operations and Algebraic Thinking
4	p. 118	Completing Number Sentences	Operations and Algebraic Thinking
5	p. 130	Length of Rope	Measurement and Data
6	p. 165	Odd Shape Out	Geometry
6	p. 170	Coloring One Half	Geometry
		Grade 2	
3	p. 79	Building Numbers	Number and Operations in Base Ten
3	p. 88	Labeling the Number Line	Number and Operations in Base Ten
3	p. 93	Are They Equivalent?	Geometry
4	p. 123	Solving Number Stories	Operations and Algebraic Thinking
5	p. 137	Comparing Measures	Measurement and Data
5	p. 143	Reading Line Plots	Measurement and Data

2

Counting and Cardinality Probes

The content of the Probes in this chapter aligns with the standards for kindergarten. All of these Probes and their variations will also be relevant for students in grades 1 and up who have not yet met these kindergarten standards.

Understanding number and having number sense in the early years involves understanding quantity, comparing quantities, fluency and flexibility with counting, and the ability to perform simple operations with numbers. The standards identify number, relations, and operations as important areas of focus for instructional time during kindergarten through second grade. Foundational to the development of these areas of focus is the development of counting, cardinality, and beginning to operate on whole numbers in kindergarten.

We developed these Probes to address this critical area of focus for kindergarten, described in the standards (CCSSO, 2010) as follows.

Representing, relating, and operating on whole numbers, initially with sets of objects

Students use numbers, including written numerals, to represent quantities and to solve quantitative problems, such as

- counting objects in a set;
- counting out a given number of objects;

> The content of the Probes in this chapter aligns with the standards for kindergarten. All of these Probes and their variations will also be relevant for students in grades 1 and up who have not yet met these kindergarten standards.

- comparing sets or numerals;
- modeling simple joining and separating situations with sets of objects, or eventually with equations such as $5 + 2 = 7$ and $7 - 2 = 5$.

The standards and their related questions, as well as the Probes associated with them, are shown in the table below.

Common Core Math Content

Common Core Mathematical Content	Related Question	Probe Name
Count to tell the number of objects. **KCC.B.4, KCC.B.5** Compare numbers. **KCC.C.6**	Do students apply counting and cardinality when comparing two sets of objects?	Chicken and Eggs (p. 29)
Know number names and the count sequence. **KCC.A.2, KCC.A.3** Count to tell the number of objects. **KCC.4b**	Do students apply counting strategies and number sense to determine the missing number(s) in a counting sequence and write the numeral to match the number name?	Name the Missing Number (p. 38)
Count to tell the number of objects. **KCC.A.3, KCC.B.4a**	Do students apply counting strategies to determine the number of dots in a collection, and can they match the quantity they have counted or calculated with its numeral?	Dots and Numerals: Card Match (p. 46)
Count to tell the number of objects. **KCC.B.4** Understand addition as putting together and adding to and subtraction as taking apart and taking from. **K.OA.1, K.OA.1.2, K.OA.B.4, K.OA.B.5**	Do students understand the concepts of cardinality and hierarchical inclusion?	Counting and Combining (p. 54)
Compare numbers between 1 and 10 presented as written numerals. **K.CC.C.7**	Are students able to choose the larger number when given only a pair of written numerals?	Comparing Numbers (p. 61)

Take a look at the variations that are available with some of the Probes in this chapter. All of these variations address counting and cardinality but may extend the idea or offer a different structure for administration. When available, variation Probes follow the Teacher Notes and associated reproducibles for the related original Probe, as shown in the table below.

Variations Chart

Probe Name	Variation Name
Name the Missing Number p. 38	Name the Missing Number 2 p. 44
Dots and Numerals: Card Match p.46	Dots and Numerals Set B p. 53
Comparing Numbers p. 61	Comparing Two-Digit Numbers p. 66

Chicken and Eggs

(Student Interview; reproducible cards and recording sheet follow on p. 30)

1. Begin by showing the student the first card (Carla and Bonnie).

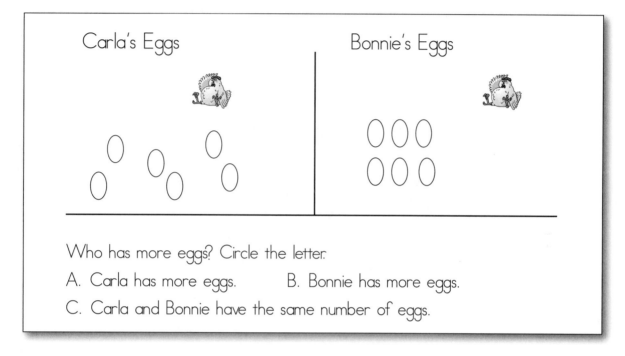

Carla's Eggs   Bonnie's Eggs

Who has more eggs? Circle the letter.
A. Carla has more eggs.   B. Bonnie has more eggs.
C. Carla and Bonnie have the same number of eggs.

2. Tell the student, *These are Carla's eggs* (pointing to Carla's eggs) *and these are Bonnie's eggs* (pointing to Bonnie's eggs).

3. Then ask, *Does Bonnie have more eggs?* (point to Bonnie's eggs) *Does Carla have more eggs?* (pointing to Carla's eggs) *Or do they have the same number of eggs?*

4. Notice what the student does to determine an answer and record notes on the recording sheet.

5. Ask the student to circle the letter that matches his/her answer or circle for the student. If it is not clear to you how the student arrived at a choice, ask questions to learn more.

6. For clarity, read the answer back to the student and point to the related visual. For example, say: *So you have answered that Carla has more eggs.*

7. Proceed to the next card and follow the same steps.

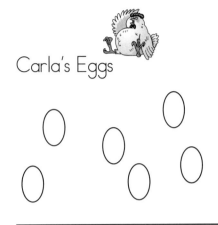

Carla's Eggs   Bonnie's Eggs

Who has more eggs? Circle the letter.

A. Carla has more eggs.   B. Bonnie has more eggs.

C. Carla and Bonnie have the same number of eggs.

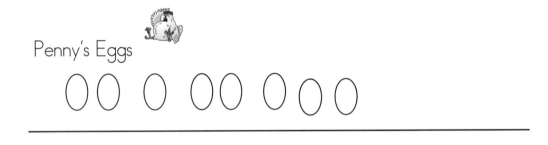

Penny's Eggs

Dee Dee's Eggs

Who has more eggs? Circle the letter.

A. Penny has more eggs.   B. Dee Dee has more eggs.

C. Penny and Dee Dee have the same number of eggs.

Nina's Eggs

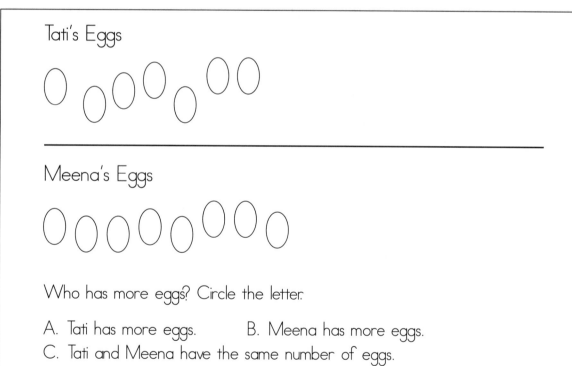

Nellie's Eggs

Who has more eggs? Circle the letter.

A. Nina has more eggs.   B. Nellie has more eggs.
C. Nina and Nellie have the same number of eggs.

Tati's Eggs

Meena's Eggs

Who has more eggs? Circle the letter.

A. Tati has more eggs.   B. Meena has more eggs.
C. Tati and Meena have the same number of eggs.

Chicken and Eggs Recording Sheet

Student's Name	Student's Choice			Notes on Student's Thinking/Approach
	Carla	Bonnie	Same	
	Penny	Dee Dee	Same	
	Nina	Nellie	Same	
	Tati	Meena	Same	
	Carla	Bonnie	Same	
	Penny	Dee Dee	Same	
	Nina	Nellie	Same	
	Tati	Meena	Same	
	Carla	Bonnie	Same	
	Penny	Dee Dee	Same	
	Nina	Nellie	Same	
	Tati	Meena	Same	
	Carla	Bonnie	Same	
	Penny	Dee Dee	Same	
	Nina	Nellie	Same	
	Tati	Meena	Same	

Teacher Notes: Chicken and Eggs

Questions to Consider About the Key Mathematical Concepts

Do students apply counting and cardinality when comparing two sets of objects? To what extent do they

- apply rote counting along with an understanding of one-to-one correspondence when they match one object in the set to one count?
- continue through a sequence of counting numbers, "1, 2, 3, 4" and so on until they've counted the whole set?
- answer the question "how many are there?" with the last number they have counted?

Common Core Connection (K.CC)

Grade: Kindergarten

Domain: Counting and Cardinality (CC)

Clusters:

B. Count to tell the number of objects.

K.CC.B.4. Understand the relationship between numbers and quantities; connect counting to cardinality.

K.CC.B.5. Count to answer "how many?" questions about as many as 20 things arranged in a line, a rectangular array, or a circle, or as many as 10 things in a scattered configuration; given a number from 1 to 20, count out that many objects.

C. Compare numbers.

K.CC.C.6. Identify whether the number of objects in one group is greater than, less than, or equal to the number of objects in another group, e.g., by using matching and counting strategies.

Uncovering Student Understanding About the Key Concepts

Using the Chicken and Eggs Probe can provide the following information about how students are thinking about counting and cardinality.

Do they

- recognize that the arrangement of a group of objects does not change the count?

OR

Do they

- think that the arrangement of the eggs determines which is greater?

Do they

- give the last number they've counted as the count of the set of objects?

OR

- apply one-to-one correspondence, applying just one counting number to each object they count?

OR

- understand how to use the count of two sets to compare them, using words such as *more* or *less?*

OR

Do they

- begin to count all over again when asked how many there are?

- skip over eggs when they are counting or double-count eggs?

- compare the size of the eggs or how they are spaced or arranged rather than the quantities?

Exploring Excerpts From Educational Resources and Related Research

Common areas of difficulty for students:

"Counting one past the actual number of items—Young children often have difficulty tagging items (touching and saying a number) and partitioning (moving aside counted items) simultaneously. This often leads to saying one extra number name." (Bay Area Mathematics Task Force, 1999, p. 10)

Misusing the acoustical sequence of numbers. Instead of counting per word (numeral) they count per syllable. For example, sev-en means 2 objects; e-lev-en means 3 objects. (Van Den Brink, 1984, p. 2)

Thinking sets of objects that are spread out have a larger count than those that are arranged close to one another. Students are "misled by perceptual clues—six items spread out may appear to be more than 7 items close together." (Bay Area Mathematics Task Force, 1999, p. 10)

When a student can count 4 objects (1, 2, 3, 4) and can answer "4" when asked "How many are there?" the student has developed cardinality. Children who understand the short cut to describing the count of a set by using the last number of the enumeration of the count (4) rather than repeating the whole count (1, 2, 3, 4) are said to have grasped the *cardinality principle.* (Gelman & Gallistel, 1978; Schaeffer, Eggleston, & Scott, 1974)

Surveying the Prompts and Selected Responses in the Probe

There are four cards, each containing two sets of objects to compare. The items are designed to elicit understandings and common difficulties as described below.

Carla and Bonnie

If a student chooses	It is likely that the student
Carla has more eggs	• thinks that the arrangement of a set of objects is related to the size or count of the set of objects (more spread out or random is larger).
Bonnie has more eggs	• counts incorrectly or has difficulty with comparison words like *same* or *more*.
Carla and Bonnie have the same number of eggs (correct answer)	• applies one-to-one correspondence and other counting strategies and is able to compare quantities using *same* and *more*.

Penny and Dee Dee

If a student chooses	It is likely that the student
Penny has more eggs	• is applying accurate counting and comparison strategies.
Dee Dee has more eggs	• has a misconception that objects that are spread out in an arrangement are "more" than objects arranged more closely to one another. (See Sample Student Response 1.)
Penny and Dee Dee have the same number of eggs	• has made a counting error such as missing or double-counting an egg.

Nina and Nellie

If a student chooses	It is likely that the student
Nina has more eggs	• has a misconception that there are more of Nina's eggs because her eggs are larger and/or more spread out than Nellie's eggs. (See Sample Student Response 2.)
Nellie has more eggs	• is applying accurate counting, subitizing, and/or comparison strategies.
Nina and Nellie have the same number of eggs	• has made a counting error or compares eggs based on visual appearance rather than counting.

Tati and Meena

If a student chooses	It is likely that the student
Tati has more eggs	• compares the sets of eggs based on sizes of eggs rather than counts. (Bigger egg is more than smaller egg.)
Meena has more eggs	• applies a correct counting approach to correctly determine the number of objects in each set. (See Sample Student Response 3.)

(Continued)

(Continued)

If a student chooses	It is likely that the student
Tati and Meena have the same number of eggs	• has made a counting error or may be using a method other than counting to compare. (For example, each set looks about the same size and is organized and spaced the same, so the two sets have the same number of eggs.)

Teaching Implications and Considerations

Ideas for eliciting more information from students about their understanding and difficulties:

- How can you tell that _____ has more eggs than _____?
- Does it matter which egg you start with when you count?
- Is there more than one way to determine who has more eggs?
- What happens when some eggs are bigger than other eggs? (Refer to Nina and Nellie or Tati and Mina card.)
- How do you count the eggs when they are in a line? In rows? In a mixed up jumble? (Refer to Carla and Bonnie and Penny and Dee Dee cards.)

Ideas for planning instruction in response to what you learned from the results of administering the Probe:

- Use concrete materials. Skill in counting is supported by providing sets of blocks or counters that students can manipulate as they are counting. These concrete materials can help to build understanding of one-to-one correspondence and provide engaging practice in matching number names with the objects being counted. Counting objects arranged in one straight row is easier for children than counting objects arranged randomly or in organized rectangular array or circles.
- Provide opportunities for students to build or draw sets of different sizes to build understanding of comparative terminology. Ask students to create two groups of counters, one that is more than the other. Give students practice building sets that fit certain criteria for comparison: the same, more or less.
- Be explicit about counting guidelines—each object must be counted once and only once—and discuss strategies for counting. How do you keep track of items you have already counted? Does it matter where you start when you are counting a set? How do you decide where to start? Do you use any shortcuts when you are counting a set of objects?
- Write numbers to show the counts of sets of objects: Students need experiences in connecting the number name with its numeral representation. Connecting the last number counted with its numeric representation can support the idea of cardinality—I count up until I've counted each object, and the last name I count is the number of objects. I can describe the count by saying or writing a number.

Sample Student Responses to Chicken and Eggs

Responses That Suggest Difficulty

Sample Student Response 1

Student: Dee Dee has more eggs than Penny.

Teacher: How do you know?

Student: Dee Dee's eggs go all the way to here (points to the last egg on the right) and Penny's go to here (points to the last egg on the right).

Teacher: How many eggs does Dee Dee have?

Student: 7

Teacher: And how many eggs does Penny have?

Student: 8

Teacher: And Dee Dee has more eggs.

Student: Yes.

Sample Student Response 2

Student: Nina has more eggs.

Teacher: Nina has more eggs than Nellie?

Student: Yes.

Teacher: How do you know?

Student: The eggs are bigger?

Teacher: Yes, the eggs are bigger. Are there more eggs here (pointing to Nina's eggs) than here (pointing to Nellie's eggs)?

Student: Yes.

Responses That Suggest Understanding

Sample Student Response 3

Student: (Pointing to Tati's eggs and counting) 1, 2, 3, 4, 5, 6, 7. 7 eggs. (Pointing to Meena's eggs and counting) 1, 2, 3, 4, 5, 6, 7, 8. 8 eggs.

Teacher: Does Tati have more eggs? Does Meena have more eggs? Or do they have the same number of eggs?

Student: Meena has more eggs.

Teacher: Why do you say Meena has more eggs?

Student: She has 8 eggs, and 8 is 1 more than 7.

Name the Missing Number

(Student Interview; reproducible cards follow Teacher Notes on p. 43.)

2.2

1. Give the student the first number strip (A). Point to the blank space and ask the student:
   What number goes in this space?
   (Observe what the student does to find an answer and record notes.)

2. Ask the student: *Can you write that number in this space?*
   (If the student is not able to write the number, write it for him or her.)

3. Repeat with the next three strips, taking the completed strip back so that students are not able to reference it when trying to complete the next strip.

4. If the student is able to successfully complete these items, continue with the next three strips.

A.	1	2		4	5	6	7	8	9	10

B.	1	2	3	4	5	6		8	9	10

C.	4	5	6	7		9	10	11	12	13

D.	10	11	12	13	14		16	17		19

E.	9	10		12		14	15	16		18

F.	20	21	22	23	24	25		27	28	29

G.	37	38	39		41	42	43	44	45	46

Teacher Notes:
Name the Missing Number

Questions to Consider About the Key Mathematical Concepts

Do students apply counting strategy and number sense to determine the missing number(s) in a counting sequence and write the numeral to match the number name? To what extent do they

- demonstrate an ability to count on from a given number?
- write missing numerals in a sequence of numbers?

Common Core Connection (K.CC)

Grade: Kindergarten

Domain: Counting and Cardinality (CC)

Cluster:

A. Know number names and the count sequence.

K.CC.A.2. Count forward beginning from a given number within the known sequence (instead of having to begin at 1).

K.CC.A.3. Write numbers from 0 to 20. Represent a number of objects with a written numeral 0-20 (with 0 representing a count of no objects).

Uncovering Student Understanding About the Key Concepts

Using the Find the Missing Number Probe can provide the following information about how students are thinking about counting and the relationship between number names and their matching numeral.

Do they
- count on accurately from 1 to a number between 1 and 20?   OR
- count on from a number other than 1?   OR
- connect numerals to their number names and vice versa?   OR
- write numerals from 1 to 40?   OR
- make transitions at "decades," such as tens, twenties, and thirties?   OR

Do they
- get stuck at a number in the sequence or skip numbers in the count between 1 and 20?
- begin back at 1 each time they count?
- have difficulty matching a number name to its numeral?
- have difficulty writing numerals?
- have difficulty transitioning to a new "decade"?

Exploring Excerpts From Educational Resources and Related Research

Common areas of difficulty for students:

"Helping children read and write the 10 single digit numerals is similar to teaching them to read and write letters of the alphabet. Neither has anything to do with number concepts." (Van de Walle, Karp, & Bay-Williams, 2013, p. 132)

"Counting on is a very difficult strategy for children to construct, because they almost have to negate their earlier strategy of counting from the beginning. And understanding *why* the strategy works depends on developing a sense of cardinality and hierarchical inclusion." (Fosnot & Dolk, 2001, pp. 36–37)

"The linguistic failure of the numeral system in English, especially around the irregular sequence of 'eleven, twelve, thirteen, fourteen and fifteen' explains many children's delays in mastery of the sequence of numerals needed for counting. Irregular is another way of saying they just do not make sense! This is in marked contrast with Welsh, Chinese, Japanese and many other languages in which the linguistic patterns support the mathematical structure with terminology such as ten-one, ten-two, and so on." (Ryan & Williams, 2007, p. 54)

"Although the forward sequence of numbers is relatively familiar to most young children, counting on from a particular number and counting back are often difficult skills." (Van de Walle et al., 2013, p. 133)

Surveying the Prompts and Selected Responses in the Probe

There are seven number strips in the collection, and they get progressively more difficult. The number strips are designed to elicit understandings and common difficulties as described below.

Number Strip	If the student has difficulty with the number strip, it is likely that the student
A	• has not yet memorized the rote counting numbers 0 to 5. • is not yet able to match numerals 1–5 to their number names. • is not able to write the numeral 3.
B	• has not yet memorized the rote counting numbers 0 to 10 or has omitted some numbers while counting. • is not yet able to match numerals 1–10 to their number names. • is not able to write the numeral 7.
C	• is not yet able to count on from a number other than 1. • is not able to write the numeral 8.

Number Strip	If the student has difficulty with the number strip, it is likely that the student
D	• is not able to write numerals greater than 10 to match their number names. (See Sample Student Response 1.) • has trouble counting on from 10. • has trouble transitioning to the teen numbers.
E	• has trouble transitioning to the teens decade. • has trouble with challenging number names like *eleven* and *thirteen*.
F	• has difficulty matching the numeral 20 to its number name. • has trouble counting on from 20. • has trouble transitioning and counting up in the twenties decade.
G	• has not learned the structure of the "decades." • has difficulty transitioning from thirties to forties. (See Sample Student Response 2.)

Teaching Implications and Considerations

Watching students completing these number strips can yield valuable insight into the development of their counting skills and number sense. In addition to listening to their counting and noting their abilities to write numerals, it is important to notice the methods that students use to complete these strips.

Ideas for eliciting more information from students about their understanding and difficulties:

• Can you tell me the name for this number (point to any number on the number strip)?
• Do you know what number comes after this number?
• Can you explain how you determined what number goes in the blank box?
• Which of these strips was the easiest for you to figure out?

If students have significant difficulty on the strips A, B and C, it's probably best to wait to give strips D–G until after instruction.

Ideas for planning instruction in response to what you learned from the results of administering the Probe:

• Provide cubes or other objects for support in counting or thinking about the sequences of numbers.
• Create shorter number strips, or include a visual representation, such as dots, on the strips along with the numerals.
• Provide practice reciting the counting numbers 1 to 20.
• Practice naming numbers and having students show the matching numeral.

For students who show solid understanding on this Probe, you might consider administering the variation Probe. This variation includes strips that focus on counting backwards and one strip that includes counting from 0.

Sample Student Responses to Number Strips

Responses That Suggest Difficulty

Sample Student Response 1

		Student says "ten"		Student says "thirteen"				Student says "seventeen"	
9	10		12		14	15	16		18

Sample Student Response 2

37	38	39	Said "thirty ten"	41	42	43	44	45	46

Teacher Preparation: Copy one page per student. Cut each page into seven separate strips.

A. | 1 | 2 | | 4 | 5 | 6 | 7 | 8 | 9 | 10 |

B. | 1 | 2 | 3 | 4 | 5 | 6 | | 8 | 9 | 10 |

C. | 4 | 5 | 6 | 7 | | 9 | 10 | 11 | 12 | 13 |

D. | 10 | 11 | 12 | 13 | 14 | | 16 | 17 | 18 | 19 |

E. | 9 | 10 | | 12 | | 14 | 15 | 16 | | 18 |

F. | 20 | 21 | 22 | 23 | 24 | 25 | | 27 | 28 | 29 |

G. | 37 | 38 | 39 | | 41 | 42 | 43 | 44 | 45 | 46 |

Variation: Name the Missing Number 2

(Student Interview; reproducible cards follow)

1. Give the student the first number strip (A). Point to the blank space and ask the student *What number goes in this space?*
   (Observe what the student does to find an answer and record notes.)

2. Ask the student: *Can you write that number in this space?*
   (If the student is not able to write the number, write it for him or her.)

3. Repeat with the next two strips.

A. | 11 | 12 | | 14 | 15 | 16 | 17 | 18 | 19 | |

B. | 10 | 9 | 8 | | 6 | 5 | 4 | 3 | 2 | 1 |

C. | | 1 | 2 | 3 | | 5 | 6 | 7 | 8 | 9 |

D. | 22 | 21 | 20 | | 18 | 17 | 16 | | 14 | 13 |

A. | 11 | 12 | | 14 | 15 | 16 | 17 | 18 | 19 | |

B. | 10 | 9 | 8 | | 6 | 5 | 4 | 3 | 2 | 1 |

C. | | 1 | 2 | 3 | | 5 | 6 | 7 | 8 | 9 |

D. | 22 | 21 | 20 | 19 | | 17 | 16 | | 14 | 13 |

Dots and Numerals: Card Match

(Matching Card reproducible for students follows Teacher Notes on p. 51)

1. Help the student lay out the numeric cards 1–10 in order face up in front of the student.

1	2	3	4	5
6	7	8	9	0

2. Place one set of shuffled picture cards face down in a stack on table

Set A

and say,

I am going to turn over a card to show you a picture of some dots. I want you to look at the picture card and quickly tell me the number of dots on the card.

3. Turn over the first dot picture card, place it on the table near the student, and ask, *How many dots are there?*

[Observe the student's method of determining the number of dots. Does the student count or subitize? If it's not clear what method the student used, ask the student to explain. How quickly is the student able to determine the count?]

4. Next, ask the student, *Can you show the number card that matches this picture?*

[Observe the student's method for finding the matching number card. Record the answers on the recording sheet.]

5. Continue with Set B at this sitting or at another time.

Teacher Notes:
Dots and Numerals: Card Match

Questions to Consider About the Key Mathematical Concepts

Do students apply counting strategies to determine the number of dots in a collection, and can they match the quantity they have counted or calculated with its numeral? To what extent do they

- apply one-to-one correspondence to counting?
- apply strategies such as subitizing (looking at a group of 3 dots and knowing there are 3 without actually counting them 1, 2, 3)?
- use subitizing in conjunction with other counting strategies, such as counting by 2s to quickly and accurately find the total number of dots in a bigger set without counting the whole set?

Common Core Connection (K.CC)

Grade: Kindergarten

Domain: Counting and Cardinality (CC)

Clusters:

A. Know number names and the count sequence.

K.CC.A.3. Write numbers from 0 to 20. Represent a number of objects with a written numeral 0–20 (with 0 representing a count of no objects).

B. Count to tell the number of objects.

K.CC.B.4. Understand the relationship between numbers and quantities; connect counting to cardinality.

a. When counting objects, say the number names in the standard order, pairing each object with one and only one number name and each number name with one and only one object.

Uncovering Student Understanding About the Key Concepts

Using the Dots and Numerals: Card Match Probe can provide information about how students are thinking about counting and cardinality.

Do they		*Do they*
• subitize small group of dots (1 to 4) and arrive at a count quickly and efficiently?	OR	• point to the dots and count them one by one in some or all of the sets?

Do they

- apply systematic methods to counting arrangements of dots?   OR
- determine counts of dots with accuracy?   OR

- use visual patterns within the dot configurations to count and combine subsets of dots to find a total count?   OR

Do they

- count in a random and unorganized fashion?
- make mistakes in their counting, such as skipping or double-counting dots?

- apply the same counting strategy on all cards even when the dot configurations on some cards allow for more efficient counting methods?

Exploring Excerpts From Educational Resources and Related Research

Common areas of difficulty for students:

Students experience more difficulty counting sets of objects that are randomly arranged than sets that are organized in a line or a rectangular array of rows and columns. (CCSSO Learning Progression, http://ime.math.arizona.edu/progressions/)

"Practice with subitizing is a fun early step in ensuring that our students are not number calling but understanding what is underneath the numeral. This connects most directly to the number sense components of quantity and different forms of number." (Cain & Faulkner, 2011, p. 292)

Students need to identify, write, and read numerals in connection to various representations with objects in order to begin to visualize the size of the quantity. "Include counting objects, fingers, and later abstract things such as years of age, and eventually represent the quantity with a numeral." (Bay Area Mathematics Task Force, 1999, p. 8)

"Children (and birds for that matter) can perceive two or three as a whole (subitize) without doing any mathematical thinking. We can perceive three objects as a group of three and know if it is more than two because it looks like more, without performing a mathematical operation on it. But, to understand that when we count to nine (a number too large to subitize) the result is nine objects, and that if one is removed there are eight objects left because eight and one more make nine, requires logical mathematical thinking." (Fosnot & Dolk, 2001, p. 36)

Surveying the Prompts and Selected Responses in the Probe

There are nine cards with dots, one blank card to represent 0, and ten matching numeral cards. The items are designed to elicit understandings and common difficulties as described below.

If a student	It is likely that the student
correctly and quickly names the number of dots on the card 1, 2, and 3 without obvious counting	• is visually subitizing. That is, the student can just tell these numbers by looking without counting.
gives a count for 5, 6, 7, or 8 without counting dots one by one	• is conceptually subitizing: sees small subsets of 1, 2, and/or 3 within the set of dots and combines these to get a total. • is adding small numbers to get a total or is subitizing and counting on. (See Sample Student Response 1.)
correctly selects numeral cards	• has learned the numeric representations for the number names 1 through 10 (and maybe also zero).
is not able to give a correct count name for a dot card	• may not understand cardinality—that the count of a set of objects is the name of the last number counted. (See Sample Student Response 3.) • may not understand one-to-one correspondence. • may have skipped or double-counted dots. (See Sample Student Response 2.)

Teaching Implications and Considerations

Ideas for eliciting more information from students about their understanding and difficulties:

- If you only observed the student performing counting of the dots one by one, ask the student if there is another way to determine the number of dots in the set of dots.
- Ask which dot cards were more difficult and which were easier to count.
- If the student mismatched counts with numerals, ask the student to read the numeral cards to you to learn which ones the student knows and doesn't know.

Ideas for planning instruction in response to what you learned from the results of administering the Probe:

- Provide concrete materials, such as counters, cubes, or tiles. Arrange the tiles in the same configurations as the Probe. Students who have difficulty correctly counting may have more success when they can move each object while they are counting it.
- Use color-coding with concrete materials or printed handouts to help students to see the subitized groups within a collection of dots.
- Limit practice to sets of dots that are organized in rows and columns. Practice matching the dot quantities with their numerals, first focusing on a subset of the numerals the student knows best, adding additional numerals as the student gains fluency matching dots with numerals.
- Practice skip-counting by 2s and 3s.

Sample Student Responses to Dots and Numerals: Card Match

Responses That Suggest Understanding

Sample Student Response 1

Teacher: (turns over the dot card with five dots and asks) How many dots are there?

Student: (promptly) 3 (then points to dots on right and counts), 4, 5
Teacher: How many dots are there?
Student: 5
Teachers: How do you know there are 5?
Student: I see 3, then 4, 5.
Teacher: Can you show the number card that matches this picture?
Student: (selects the 5 card and shows it to the teacher)

Responses That Suggest Difficulty

Sample Student Response 2

Teacher: (turns over the dot card with 6 dots and asks) How many dots are there?

Student: (starts to count from top left corner, 1, 2; then counts down, double-counting the corner dot: 3, 4, 5; then continues across the bottom, 6, 7 and up 8, 9, 10)
Teacher: How many dots are there?
Student: 10
Teacher: Can you show the number card that matches this picture?
Student: (selects the 10 card) It's this one.

Sample Student Response 3

Teacher: (turns over the dot card with 5 dots and asks) How many dots are there?

Student: (starts pointing and counting) 1, 2, 3, 4, 5
Teacher: How many dots are there?
Student: (counts again) 1, 2, 3, 4, 5
Teacher: Can you show the number card that matches this picture?
Student: I don't know. It might be this one (shows the 6 card).

1	2	3	4	5
6	7	8	9	0

Dots and Numerals Set A

2.3a

Dots and Numerals Recording Sheet

Image	Number Student Named	Numeral Card Selected	Image	Number Student Named	Numeral Card Selected
▫ (1 dot)			▫ (6 dots)		
▫ (2 dots)			▫ (7 dots)		
▫ (3 dots)			▫ (8 dots)		
▫ (4 dots)			▫ (9 dots)		
▫ (5 dots)			▫ (empty)		

Dots and Numerals Set B

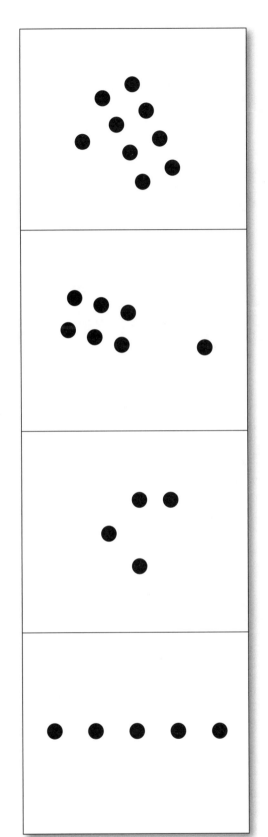

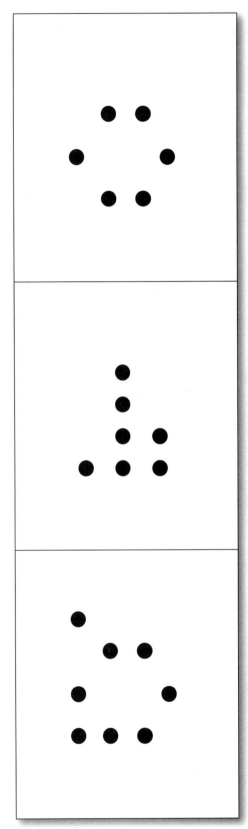

Counting and Combining

(Student Interview; reproducible mat and recording
sheet follow Teacher Notes on pp. 59–60.)

Place a mixed collection of counters, made up of exactly 4 yellow counters, 3 red counters, 5 green counters, and 2 blue counters in front of the child.

Question Set 1
Put the 4 yellow counters on the mat. *a. Please count the yellow counters.* *b. How many yellow counters are there?*
Question Set 2
Put the 3 yellow counters and 2 red counters on the mat. *c. How many counters are on the mat?* *d. Please bring the green counters on the mat with the yellow and red counters. Now how many counters are on the mat?*
Question Set 3
Put the 4 green counters and the 1 blue counter on the mat. *e. Are there more green counters or more blue counters?* *f. How many more?*
Question Set 4
Put 4 yellow counters and 3 red counters on the mat. *g. How many counters are on the mat?* *h. How many more counters are needed to have 10 counters on the mat? Show me.*
Question Set 5
Put 3 red counters and 2 blue counters on the mat. *i. How many counters are on the mat?* *j. How many more counters are needed to have 10 counters on the mat? Show me.*

Source: Adapted from Rowley, Gervasoni, Clarke, Horne, & McDonough (2001).

Teacher Notes:
Counting and Combining

Questions to Consider About the Key Mathematical Concepts

Do students understand the concepts of cardinality and hierarchical inclusion? To what extent do they

- name the last number counted as the number of objects in a set?
- apply the concept of hierarchical inclusion (understand that the quantity 6 contains 5 plus 1 more)?

Common Core Connection (K.CC and K.OA)

Grade: Kindergarten

Domain: Counting and Cardinality (CC)

Clusters:

B. Count to tell the number of objects.

K.CC.B.4. Understand the relationship between numbers and quantities; connect counting to cardinality.

A. Understand addition as putting together and adding to, and understand subtraction as taking apart and taking from.

K.OA.A.1. Represent addition and subtraction with objects, fingers, mental images, drawings, sounds (e.g., claps), acting out situations, verbal explanations, expressions, or equations.

K.OA.A.2. Solve addition and subtraction word problems, and add and subtract within 10, for example, by using objects or drawings to represent the problem.

K.OA.A.4. For any number from 1 to 9, find the number that makes 10 when added to the given number, for example, by using objects or drawings, and record the answer with a drawing or equation.

Uncovering Student Understanding About the Key Concepts

Using the Counting and Combining Probe can provide the following information about how the students are thinking about determining how many are in a set.

Do they
- create a set of counters that match a given a total?

OR

Do they
- bring the wrong number of counters onto the mat?

Do they		*Do they*
• give the last number they've counted as the count of the set of objects?	OR	• begin to count all over again when asked how many there are?
• count on to determine the total number of counters when two sets are combined?	OR	• count all, beginning at 1?
• determine how many more counters of one color there are as compared to a set of a different color?	OR	• have difficulty finding the difference?
• determine how many more counters are needed to reach a given number?	OR	• give the total number of counters on the mat?

Exploring Excerpts From Educational Resources and Related Research

Common areas of difficulty for students:

The development of counting follows a learning trajectory. As learning progresses, examples of how students' understanding builds include

- reciting numbers words; difficulties at this stage include incorrect order, saying more words than items, and skipping objects.
- having one-to-one correspondence; difficulties at this stage include counting all objects again when asked "how many?"
- producing a correct quantity when asked to count out a number of objects.

The above stages among others are important foundations to stages focusing on counting from any number. (Clements & Sarama, 2009)

"Although the forward sequence of numbers is relatively familiar to most young children, counting on from a particular number and counting back are often difficult skills." (Van de Walle et al., 2013, p. 133)

The primary reason for difficulties with counting objects (skipping objects or double-tagging) is that students have not yet constructed the big idea of cardinality. To know that the number you say tells the quantity you have, and that the number you end on when counting represents the entire amount, involve cardinality. (Fosnot & Dolk, 2001, p. 33)

Understanding the strategy of counting on to determine a total number of objects requires students to have a sense of "hierarchical inclusion—the idea that numbers build exactly one each time and that they nest within each other by this amount." (Fosnot & Dolk, 2001, p. 36)

Surveying the Prompts and Selected Responses in the Probe

There are five question sets, each with two questions. The prompts are designed to elicit understandings and common difficulties as described below.

If a student chooses	It is likely that the student
correct responses to questions a, b, c, g, and i	• understands cardinality. The student can name the total after counting or subitizing.
incorrect responses to questions a, b, c, g, and i	• is unable to count the objects, lacks one-to-one correspondence, or • is recounting the objects thinking the act of counting is the answer to "how many." (See Sample Student Response 1.)
correct responses to questions d, f, h, and j	• is applying hierarchy of inclusion to determine response by counting on, or • is able to successfully count all to determine a total.

incorrect responses to questions d, f, h, and j	• is doing one of the following:
	   o incorrect counting on
	   o counting on past a total of 10 (h and j)
	   o combining rather than comparing (See Sample Student Response 2.)

Teaching Implications and Considerations

Ideas for eliciting more information from students about their understanding and difficulties:

- For students who count again to answer "how many": Try rephrasing the question by asking, "What is the total number of objects on the mat?"
- For students who have difficulty with one-to-one correspondence due to disorganization of counters: Ask the student to line up the counters and count again.
- For students who have difficulty answering "how many more to 10": Provide a ten-frame for students to use as an organizer.

Ideas for planning instruction in response to what you learned from the results of administering the Probe:

- As students are playing a variety of counting games or involved in a variety of counting activities, ask probing questions related to "how many more" within the natural context of the current task at hand.
- Use of organizing structures such as the ten-frame can help students answer the question "how many more to 10?"

- "Use of routines by themselves does not automatically produce learning. Children who do not understand cardinality are merely being led to count to the teacher's answer, and children who have constructed concepts of cardinality and hierarchal inclusion likely do not need the activities. Teachers need to turn these counting situations into real, open dilemmas that need to be modeled and solved." (Fosnot & Dolk, 2001, pp. 41–42)

- Once students develop a concept of cardinality, little more is gained from simple counting activities. Building three additional types of number relations to further number sense is a good next step. These include *1 or 2 more* and *1 or 2 less* to push understanding of merely counting on or counting back by ones; *5 or 10 as benchmarks* to begin to understand the importance of 10 in the number system; and *part-part-whole relationships* to help students conceptualize a number as having one or more parts. (Van de Walle, Karp, & Bay-Williams, 2013, p. 136)

Sample Student Responses to Counting and Combining

Responses That Suggest Difficulty

Sample Student Response 1

Teacher: (from Question Set 2 c) How many counters are on the mat?

Student: 1, 2, 3, 4, 5 (counts yellow and red counters)

Teacher: How many counters are on the mat?

Student: 1, 2, 3, 4, 5 (counts yellow and red counters)

Teacher: What is the total number of counters on the mat?

Student: 1, 2, 3, 4, 5 (counts yellow and red counters)

Sample Student Response 2

Teacher: (Question Set 4 h) How many more counters are needed to have 10 counters on the mat?

Student: (Adds 5 more yellow counters and 5 more red counters keeping the new counters separate from the first 7 counters; counts) 8, 9, 10, 11, 12, 13, 14, 15, 16, 17

Teacher: How many counters are on the mat?

Student: 17

Teacher: What if you can only have 10 counters on the mat? How many of these (points to group of 10) should you take off the mat?

Student: (takes away 5 yellow)

Responses That Suggest Understanding

Sample Student Response 3

Teacher: (Question Set 3 e) Are there more green counters or more blue counters?

Student: Green

Teacher: How many more green?

Student: (creates rows and matches 1 blue and 1 green, and moves the pair of counters to the side) 3

Work Mat for Counting and Combining

2.4b

Counting and Combining Recording Sheet

Name	Set 1		Set 2		Set 3		Set 4		Set 5		Notes

Comparing Numbers

2.5

Circle the Bigger Number	
A. 6 9	Tell or Show Why
B. 8 7	Tell or Show Why
C. 9 4	Tell or Show Why
D. 8 10	Tell or Show Why

Teacher Notes: Comparing Numbers

Questions to Consider About the Key Mathematical Concepts

Are students able to choose the larger number when given only a pair of written numerals? To what extent do they

- understand magnitude; have a sense of a quantity as a specific amount?
- have a sense of one quantity in relationship to the other quantity when comparing two numbers?

Common Core Connection (K.CC)

Grade: Kindergarten

Domain: Counting and Cardinality (CC)

Cluster:

C. Compare numbers.

K.CC.C.7. Compare two numbers between 1 and 10 presented as written numerals.

Uncovering Student Understanding About the Key Concepts

Using the Comparing Numbers Probe can provide the following information about how the students are thinking about the magnitude of numbers.

Do they		*Do they*
• name the number shown?	OR	• ask what the number is?
• visualize the quantities without needing objects or tools?	OR	• need support in representing the number?
		• focus on the size of the symbol rather than the quantity it represents?
• correctly compare the two given numbers?	OR	• make a mistake when determining which number is larger?
• explain why one number is larger than the other?	OR	• respond with a nonnumeric explanation?

Note on the use of counters: When giving a student a counting task, have counters ready but only for students who ask for them, or to give to students who show frustration about being unable to solve the task without physical objects. Students may also ask for other resources they have used previously when solving similar tasks, such as ten-frames and number lines. Given the diagnostic nature of the task, refrain from suggesting the use of such tools, but make them available if a student specifically asks to use a particular tool.

Exploring Excerpts From Educational Resources and Related Research

Common areas of difficulty for students:

"Helping children read and write numerals is similar to teaching them to read and write letters of the alphabet. Neither has anything to do with number concepts. Numeral writing does not have to be repetitious practice." (Van de Walle, Karp, & Bay-Williams, 2013, p. 133)

Teaching number words and symbols is deceptively difficult. "Take the numeral 3. Just as *c-a-t* is not a cat, the numeral 3 is not the quantity three. *T-h-r-e-e* is not three either. Three dots, . . . , are a little closer to the reality, just as a picture of a cat (see fig. 2) is a bit closer to a real cat. But if the numeral 3, the word *three* and . . . are not three, what *is* three? . . . We must first ascertain that students 'see' number in a way that will engender their understanding of compositions and decompositions of number (Clements and Sarama 2009). Only this will allow students to truly read number." (Cain & Faulkner, 2011, pp. 290–291)

Students first learn to match the objects in the two groups to see if there are any extra in one group or the other, and then to count the objects in each group and use their knowledge of the count sequence to decide which number is greater than the other (the number farther along in the count sequence). (Common Core Standards Writing Team, 2011a, p. 5)

Surveying the Prompts and Selected Responses in the Probe

The Probe consists of four items. The prompts and selected responses are designed to elicit understandings and common difficulties as described below.

If a student chooses	It is likely that the student
correct answers (a) 9, (b) 8, (c) 9, and (d) 10	• relates the numeral to a quantity. • is able to determine the larger quantity.
incorrect response on a or c	• has reversed the related quantity, given the similar features of the two numerals. (See Sample Student Response 1.)
other incorrect responses	• has one or more of the following difficulties: ○ focusing on the size of the numeral rather than on the quantity it represents (See Sample Student Response 2.)

If a student chooses	*It is likely that the student*
	o naming the numeral incorrectly and using that quantity to compare (See Sample Student Response 3.) o incorrectly counting when using objects to determine answer choice o thinking about count sequence in opposite direction

Teaching Implications and Considerations

Ideas for eliciting more information from students about their understanding and difficulties:

- Determine if the student is reading the numerals correctly.
- If a student did not ask for counters, provide the counters, and ask the student to use the counters to check on their work.
- If students used counters but gave one or more incorrect answers, provide an organizing tool, such as a ten-frame or egg carton.
- If students answer correctly, be sure to follow up on explanations by asking, "How do you know ___ is the bigger number?"

  o If students struggle, ask "Can you show me with these counters?"
  o If students refer to the bigger number as coming after when counting, ask, "Why is it bigger if it comes after when counting?"

Ideas for planning instruction in response to what you learned from the results of administering the Probe:

- Provide multiple opportunities for students to model quantities with objects, breaking apart one quantity in multiple ways.
- Connect count-on and count-back activities to numbers that are "more" and numbers that are "less."
- Students need to identify, write, and read numerals in connection to various representations with objects in order to begin to visualize the size of the quantity. "Include counting objects, fingers, and later abstract things such as years of age, and eventually represent the quantity with a numeral." (Bay Area Mathematics Task Force, 1999, p. 8)
- "Practice with subitizing is a fun early step in ensuring that our students are not number calling but understanding what is underneath the numeral. This connects most directly to the number sense components of quantity and different forms of number." (Cain & Faulkner, 2011, p. 292)
- Use organizing tools such as ten-frames or egg cartons that allow students to see which quantity "fills up" the container more.

Sample Student Responses to Comparing Numbers

Responses That Suggest Difficulty

Sample Student Response 1
Item (a)

    Student: (circles 6)
    Teacher: Tell me why you circled this number.
    Student: It's 9, and that one is 6.

Sample Student Response 2
Item (b)

    Student: (circles 8)
    Teacher: Tell me why you circled this number.
    Student: 8 has big circles, and 7 just has two lines.

Sample Student Response 3
Item (b)

    Student: (circles 7)
    Teacher: Tell me why you circled this number.
    Student: (points to 8) This is 3 and this is 7.

Responses That Suggest Understanding

Sample Student Response 4
Item (b)

    Student: (circles 8)
    Teacher: Tell me why you circled this number.
    Student: 8 is 1 more than 7.

Comparing Two-Digit Numbers

Circle the Bigger Number	
A. 13 18	Tell or Show Why
B. 14 11	Tell or Show Why
C. 19 18	Tell or Show Why
D. 12 20	Tell or Show Why

3

Number and Operations in Base Ten Probes

The content of the Probes in this chapter aligns with the number and operations in base-ten standards for grades 1 and 2. The Probes and their variations will also be relevant for kindergarteners who have met their grade-level standards.

We developed these Probes to address the critical areas of focus in number and operations in base ten for grades 1 and 2, described in the standards (CCSSO, 2010) as

Grade 1: Developing understanding of whole number relationships and place value, including grouping in tens and ones

Students

- compare whole numbers (at least to 100) to develop understanding of and solve problems involving their relative sizes.
- think of whole numbers between 10 and 100 in terms of tens and ones (especially recognizing the numbers 11 to 19 as composed of a ten and some ones).
- understand the order of the counting numbers and their relative magnitudes.

> The content of the Probes in this chapter aligns with the number and operations in base-ten standards for grades 1 and 2. The Probes and their variations will also be relevant for kindergarteners who have met their grade-level standards.

Grade 2: Extending understanding of base-ten notation

Students

- extend their understanding of the base-ten system.
- understand multidigit numbers (up to 1,000) written in base-ten notation (e.g., 853 is 8 hundreds + 5 tens + 3 ones).

The standards and their related questions, as well as the Probes associated with them, are shown in the table below.

Common Core Math Content

Common Core Mathematical Content	Related Question	Probe Name
Understand place value. **1.NBT.B.2**	Do students apply a key place value understanding that the location of a digit in a number tells you about its quantity?	What's the Value of the Digit? (p. 69)
Understand place value. **2.NBT.A.1**	When writing a number, do students use their understanding of place value rather than just building numbers based on the order of the digits as provided?	Building Numbers (p. 79)
Develop understanding of fractions as numbers. **3.NF.A.2**	Are students able to locate and label points on the number line?	Labeling the Number Line (p. 88)
Use place value understanding and properties of operations to add subtract. **2.NBT.B.7, 2.NBT.B.9**	Do students understand that the placement of a digit within a number determines its value, and can they apply that understanding to determining equivalent expressions in addition and subtraction?	Are They Equivalent? (p. 93)

Take a look at the variations that are available with some of the Probes in this chapter. All of these variations address number concepts and either extend the idea or offer a different structure for administering them. When available, you'll find variation Probes after the Teacher Notes and associated reproducibles for the related original Probe, as shown in the table below.

Probe Variation Chart

Probe Name	Variation Name
What's the Value of the Digit? p. 69	Student Interview: What's the Value of the Digit? p. 76
Building Numbers p. 79	Building Numbers 2 p. 85 Building Numbers Game p. 87
Are They Equivalent? p. 93	Are They Equivalent? Three-Digit p. 99

What's the Value of the Digit?

(Student Interview; reproducible cards follow Teacher Notes on p. 75)

Card #1: Shoes

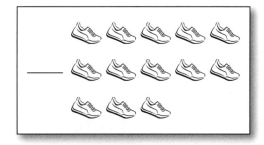

Teacher says: *There are thirteen shoes in this picture.*

Teacher points to the blank line and asks: *Can you write the number thirteen on this line?* (If the student cannot write the number or writes it incorrectly, teacher writes it for the student.)

Teacher gives the student a colored pencil, points to the number in the ones place (3), and asks: *What number is this?* (Teacher records student's response.)

Teacher continues to point at the number in the ones place (3) and asks: *Can you use your colored pencil to circle in the picture what this digit in thirteen means?* (Teacher records notes about what the student says and does.)

Card #2: Teddy Bears

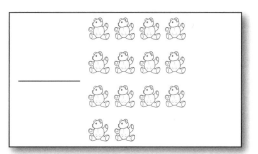

Teacher says: *There are seventeen teddy bears in this picture.*

Teacher points to the blank line and asks: *Can you write the number seventeen on this line?* (If the student cannot write the number or writes it incorrectly, write it for the student.)

Teacher gives the student a colored pencil, points to the digit in the tens place (1) and asks: *What number is this?* (Record student's response.)

Teacher continues to point at the number in the tens place (1) and asks: *Can you use your colored pencil to circle in the picture what this number in seventeen means?* (Record notes about what the student says and does.)

Card #3: Beach Ball

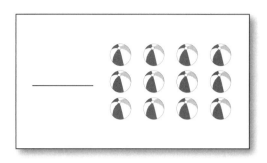

Teacher says: *There are twelve beach balls in this picture.*

Teacher points to the blank line and asks: *Can you write the number twelve on this line?* (If the student cannot write the number or writes it incorrectly, teacher writes it for the student.)

Teacher gives the student a colored pencil, points to the number in the ones place (2), and asks: *What number is this?* (Teacher records student's response.)

Teacher continues to point at the number in the ones place (2) and asks: *Can you use your colored pencil to circle in the picture what this digit in twelve means?* (Teacher records notes about what the student says and does.)

Teacher gives the child a different colored pencil, points to the number in the tens place (1), and asks: *What number is this?* (Teacher records student's response.)

Teacher continues to point at the number in the tens place (1) and asks: *Can you use your colored pencil to circle in the picture what this digit in twelve means?*

(Teacher records notes about what the student says and does.)

Teacher Notes:
What's the Value of the Digit?

Questions to Consider About the Key Mathematical Concepts

Do students apply a key place value understanding that the location of a digit in a number tells you about its quantity? To what extent do they

- compose and decompose a two-digit number into its tens and ones?
- apply one-to-one correspondence, subitizing, and skip-counting strategies?
- connect numeric values, number names, and the quantity they represent?

Common Core Connection (1.NBT)

Grade: First

Domain: Number and Operations in Base Ten (NBT)

Cluster:

B. Understand place value.

1.NBT.B.2. Understand that the two digits of a two-digit number represent amounts of tens and ones. Understand the following as special cases:

- a. 10 can be thought of as a bundle of ten ones—called a "ten."
- b. The numbers from 11 to 19 are composed of a ten and one, two, three, four, five, six, seven, eight, or nine ones.

Uncovering Student Understanding About the Key Concepts

Using the What's the Value of the Digit? Probe can provide information about how the student is thinking about key place value ideas.

Do they

- determine the value of the digit 1 by paying attention to its place value location (e.g., a one in the tens place has a value of ten)?

OR

- recognize and write numerals and their number names?

OR

Do they

- think that the digit 1 always has a value of 1 (e.g., a one has a value of one even when it is in the tens place)?

- have trouble translating between numerals and their number names and/or writing numerals?

Do they

- accurately count objects using one-to-one correspondence?

OR

- use more advanced strategies such as skip-counting or subitizing?

OR

Do they

- use flawed counting methods such as skipping or double-counting an object?

- count objects one by one only?

Exploring Excerpts From Educational Resources and Related Research

Common areas of difficulty for students:

Even students who can count and identify numbers often have difficulty with positional knowledge and digit correspondence activities. (Hanich, Jordan, Kaplan, & Dick, 2001, p. 623)

A number of researchers have found that large percentages of children even as old as fourth grade fail to recognize that the 2 in 25 represents 20 objects. (Hiebert & Wearne, 1992; Kamii, 1986; Ross, 1989).

Number knowledge extends to understanding how numbers can be composed or decomposed. "This is a foundation for part–whole understanding. . . . Students who are comfortable manipulating quantities informally in this way, and who count objects comfortably by 2s or 5s, are prepared for efficiently learning the operations of addition and subtraction and understanding them conceptually." (Bay Area Mathematics Task Force, 1999, p. 8)

Surveying the Prompts and Selected Responses in the Probe

The Probe consists of three cards with visual representations of the numbers 13, 17, and 12, and students are asked to circle quantities to match the digits in these numbers. The items are designed to elicit understandings and common difficulties as described below.

If a student	It is likely that the student
incorrectly writes the number	has not learned the number names and their matching numeric representations; these difficulties could be related to the structure and language of the teens numbers.
circles only one object to represent the value of the digit 1 in 13, 17, 12	does not understand that the digit 1 has a value of ten when it is located in the tens place. (See Sample Student Response 1.)

If a student	It is likely that the student
circles more or less than 3 shoes *or* more or less than 2 beach balls	has trouble decomposing 13 to 10 and 3, and 12 to 10 and 2. (See Sample Student Response 2.) These difficulties may be related to the challenging language of "twelve" and "thirteen" and/or to place value understanding.

The variation of this Probe includes teen numbers that are more manageable to decompose and write: 14, 19, and 18. These cards may provide some additional useful information, particularly for those students who appear to have difficulty translating the number names in this Probe to their written numeric value.

Teaching Implications and Considerations

Ideas for eliciting more information from students about their understanding and difficulties:

- Ask students if they can represent the given number with a collection of objects such as counters or straws. Ask them if they can group those objects to show the number.
- Ask place value questions that go beyond "which digit is in the ___ place?" For example, ask how many tens are in the number 54. Ask what the value of the digit 5 is in this number. Ask these place value questions only after the original questions provided in the directions.
- Notice if students are using number names correctly as they are working. Ask them to say aloud what they are doing as they circle the objects.

Ideas for planning instruction in response to what you learned from the results of administering the Probe:

- Provide many opportunities for students to use physical models such as straws, interlocking cubes, and counters to represent a two- or a three-digit number in multiple ways.
- Introduce groupable models (individual units such as straws that can be bundled together) first, and then introduce proportionally pre-grouped models (such as base-ten blocks). Models play a key role in helping students understand 10 ones as "ten" as well as 10 tens as "hundred." (Van de Walle, Karp, & Bay-Williams, 2013, p. 195)
- Provide students with experiences in noting how concrete representations of a number differ from numeric representations. Especially important is understanding that the arrangements of the digits in the numeric representation matters (the digit in the tens place is to the left

of the digit in the ones place), whereas when concrete models are used, the value is not determined by the arrangement of the materials. (NCTM, 2000, p. 81)

- For students who have errors related to counting, provide concrete objects and ask them to model the situation with the objects. Students who are using one-to-one correspondence in counting may find it helpful to move objects to accurately determine the count.

Sample Student Responses to What's the Value of the Digit?

Responses That Suggest Difficulty

Sample Student Response 1

This student circles all 13 shoes when asked to circle what 3 in 13 means.

Sample Student Response 2

This student individually circles 7 teddy bears to show the 7 in 17; then, the student circles 1 more bear to represent the 1 in 17.

Responses That Suggest Understanding

Sample Student Response 3

Thirteen Shoes

Seventeen Teddy Bears

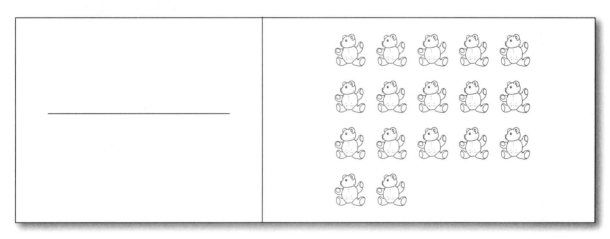

Twelve Beach Balls

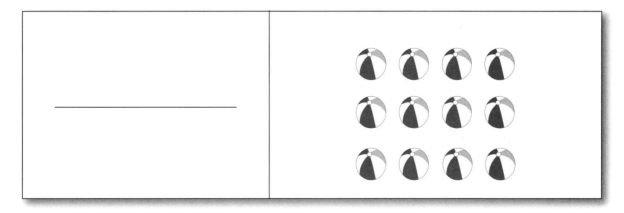

Student Interview: What's the Value of the Digit?

Card #1: Tennis Shoes

Teacher says: *There are fourteen tennis shoes in this picture.*

Teacher points to the blank line and asks: *Can you write the number fourteen on this line?* (If the student cannot write the number or writes it incorrectly, teacher writes it for the student.)

Teacher gives the child a colored pencil, points to the number in the ones place (4), and asks: *What number is this?* (Teacher records student's response.)

Teacher continues to point at the number in the ones place and asks: *Can you use your colored pencil to circle what this digit in fourteen means in the picture?* (Teacher records notes about what the student says and does.)

Card #2: Umbrellas

Teacher says: *There are nineteen umbrellas in this picture.*

Teacher points to the blank line and asks: *Can you write the number nineteen on this line?* (If the student cannot write the number or writes it incorrectly, teacher writes it for the student.)

Teacher gives the child a colored pencil, points to the digit in the tens place (1) and asks: *What number is this?* (Teacher records student's response.)

Teacher continues to point at the number in the tens place (1) and asks: *Can you use your colored pencil to circle what this digit in nineteen means in the picture?*

(Teacher records notes about what the student says and does.)

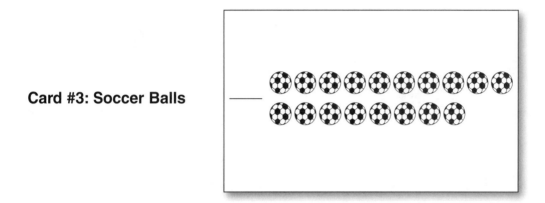

Card #3: Soccer Balls

Teacher says: *There are eighteen soccer balls in this picture.*

Teacher points to the blank line and asks: *Can you write the number eighteen on this line?* (If the student cannot write the number or writes it incorrectly, teacher writes it for the student.)

Teacher gives the child a colored pencil, points to the number in the ones place (eight) and asks: *What number is this?* (Teacher records student's response.)

Teacher continues to point at the number in the ones place and asks: *Can you use your colored pencil to circle in the picture what this digit in eighteen means?*

(Teacher records notes about what the student says and does.)

Teacher gives the child a different colored pencil, points to the number in the tens place (1), and asks: *What number is this?* (Teacher records student's response.)

Teacher continues to point at the number in the tens place and asks: *Can you use your colored pencil to circle in the picture what this digit in the number eighteen means?* (Teacher records notes about what the student says and does.)

Fourteen Tennis Shoes

Nineteen Umbrellas

Eighteen Soccer Balls

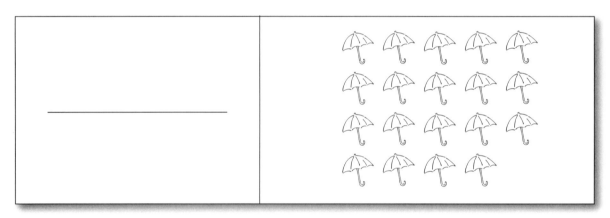

Building Numbers

3.2

Determine the number that goes in each blank (?) in the problems below.

A. 561 = | 6 | TENS + | 1 | ONE + | ? | HUNDREDS

     (is the same as)

Circle One: A. 0   B. 5   C. 1

Explain your choice:

B. 720 = | 10 | ONES + | ? | TENS + | 7 | HUNDREDS

     (is the same as)

Circle One: A. 2   B. 7   C. 1

Explain your choice:

C. ⬚? = 21 ONES + 5 TENS + 8 HUNDREDS

(is the same as)

Circle One: A. 2,158   B. 826   C. 871   D. 8,521

Explain your choice:

D. ⬚? = 6 HUNDREDS + 9 ONES + 24 TENS

(is the same as)

Circle One: A. 6,249   B. 6,924   C. 633   D. 849

Explain your choice:

Teacher Notes: Building Numbers

Questions to Consider About the Key Mathematical Concepts

When writing a number, do students use their understanding of place value rather than just building numbers based on the order of the digits as provided? To what extent do they

- compose and recompose numbers based on different place value combinations?
- model such numbers using a variety of materials and other representations?

Common Core Connection (2.NBT)

Grade: Second

Domain: Numbers and Operations in Base Ten (NBT)

Cluster:

A. Understand place value

2.NBT.A.1. Understand that the three digits of a three-digit number represent amounts of hundreds, tens, and ones; e.g., 706 equals 7 hundreds, 0 tens, and 6 ones. Understand the following as special cases:

- 100 can be thought of as a bundle of ten tens — called a "hundred."
- The numbers 100, 200, 300, 400, 500, 600, 700, 800, 900 refer to one, two, three, four, five, six, seven, eight, or nine hundreds (and 0 tens and 0 ones).

Uncovering Student Understanding About the Key Concepts

Using the Building Numbers Probe can provide the following information about how the students are thinking about place value.

Do they

- pay attention to the place value groupings of ones, tens, and hundreds?

OR

Do they

- use the numbers in the order that is shown?

- regroup when there are more than ten ones or ten tens?

OR

- rely on just the number of ones, tens, and hundreds without considering the need for regrouping?

Exploring Excerpts From Educational Resources and Related Research

Common areas of difficulty for students:

The use of *ten* as a singular group name is confusing to students. Equally confusing is the word *hundred,* which needs to be understood in multiple ways, including 100 single objects, 10 tens, and as a singular thing. These different meanings of *hundred* often get less attention than the multiple meanings of *ten.* (Van de Walle et al., 2013, p. 199)

Learning Pitfall: "Depending on order, rather than quantities, when writing a number for a collection of base ten materials." (Bay Area Mathematics Task Force, 1999, p. 11)

Even students who can count and identify numbers often have difficulty with positional knowledge and digit correspondence activities. (Hanich et al., 2001, p. 623)

"Unlike the decade words, the hundred words indicate base-ten units. For example, it takes interpretation to understand that 'fifty' means five tens, but 'five hundred' means almost what it says ('five hundred' rather than 'five hundreds'). Even so, this doesn't mean that students automatically understand 500 as 5 hundreds; they may still only think of it as the number reached after 500 counts of 1." (Common Core Standards Writing Team, 2011c, p. 8)

Surveying the Prompts and Selected Responses in the Probe

There are two items per page for a total of four items. The prompts and selected responses are designed to elicit understandings and common difficulties as described below:

If a student chooses	*It is likely that the student*
• (a) B. 5, • (b) C. 1, • (c) C. 871, *or* • (d) D. 849 (correct answers)	• pays attention to the place value groupings of ones, tens, and hundreds, and • regroups when there are more than 10 ones or 10 tens.
• (a) C. 1 *or* • (b) A. 2 (incorrect answers)	• is not paying attention to 10 tens or 10 ones and is instead using a literal "what is the digit in the ___ place" translation. (See Sample Student Response 1.)
• (c) A. 2,158 *or* • (d) B. 6,924	• is not paying attention to the place value groupings of ones, tens, and hundreds, and instead is writing the number in the order of the digits provided. (See Sample Student Response 2.)

If a student chooses	It is likely that the student
• (other incorrect answers)	• incorrectly regroups when there are more than 10 ones or 10 tens. (See Sample Student Response 3.)

Teaching Implications and Considerations

Ideas for eliciting more information from students about their understanding and difficulties:

- For those who choose "direct translation" responses, determine whether ordering and regrouping are issues by first pointing out the order and providing an opportunity to re-examine the choices.
    - o For items (a) and (b), focus on the regrouping of the 10 ones and/or 10 tens, and then provide an opportunity to re-examine the choices. Ask, Can you tell me what these (point to the 10 tens or 10 ones statements) tell you about the number of tens/ones?
    - o For items (c) and (d), focus on the regrouping of the ones and/or tens, and then provide an opportunity to re-examine the choices. Ask, Can you tell me what these (point to the number of tens or number of ones statements) tell you about the number of tens/ones?

Consider the following instructional implications when planning next steps:

- Use physical models: Introduce groupable models (individual units such as straws that can be bundled together) first, and then introduce proportionally pregrouped models (such as base-ten blocks). Models play a key role in helping students understand 10 ones as "ten" as well as 10 tens as "hundred." (Van de Walle et al., 2013, p. 195)
- Provide many opportunities for students to use physical models to represent a two- or a three-digit number in multiple ways. Students should be required to justify why the representations are equivalent.
- Provide students with experiences in noting how concrete representations of a number differ from numeric representations. Especially important is understanding that the arrangements of the digits in the numeric representation matters (the digit in the tens place is to the left of the digit in the ones place), whereas when concrete models are used, the value is not determined by the arrangement of the materials. (NCTM, 2000, p. 81)
- Ask place value questions that go beyond "which digit is in the ___ place?" For example, ask how many tens are in the number 230. Rather than always giving the number to be represented, give open ended prompts, such as this: If 14 base-ten blocks were used to create a number, what number could it be? (Small, 2009, pp. 28–29)

Sample Student Responses to Building Numbers

Responses That Suggest Difficulty

Sample Student Response 1:

(b) A. Look at the second number to find numbers of tens.

Sample Student Response 2:

(d) D. Write the numbers down, and then put a comma in.

Responses That Suggest Understanding

Sample Student Response 3:

(a) 5. Use flats, longs, and cubes. 10 longs is like a flat, so there are no longs.

Sample Student Response 4:

(c) 871. Start with 21 ones. This is 20 and 1. 50 more is 70 and 1. 800 more is 871.

Building Numbers 2

Determine whether each statement is true or false and explain.

A. [9] TENS + [2] HUNDREDS + [4] ONES < [924]

(is less than)

Circle One: TRUE   FALSE

Explain your choice:

B. [347] > [2] HUNDREDS + [52] TENS + [8] ONES

(is greater than)

Circle One: TRUE   FALSE

Explain your choice:

C. [10] TENS + [4] HUNDRED + [2] ONES > [439]

(is greater than)

Circle One: TRUE   FALSE

Explain your choice:

D. [399] < [3] HUNDREDS + [9] TENS + [19] ONES

(is less than)

Circle One: TRUE   FALSE

Explain your choice:

Building Numbers Game

Juan, Peter and Trish were playing a card game. For each hand, they each drew one card from each of three piles: the ones, tens, and hundreds piles. The person whose cards represented the largest number collected all of the cards from the other players and won that hand. The cards Juan, Peter and Trish drew are shown below.

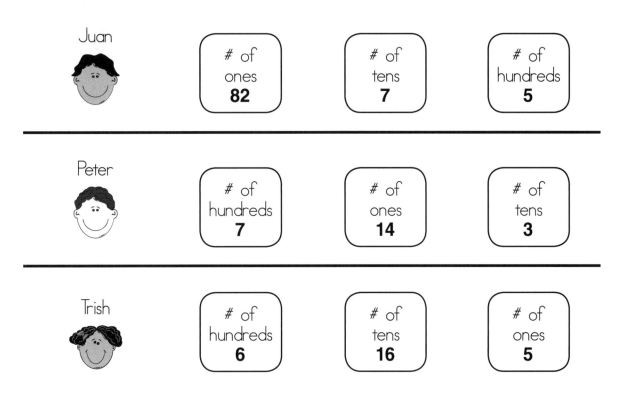

Juan
# of ones **82**   # of tens **7**   # of hundreds **5**

Peter
# of hundreds **7**   # of ones **14**   # of tens **3**

Trish
# of hundreds **6**   # of tens **16**   # of ones **5**

Circle the name of the student who has the largest number. Explain your thinking.

Labeling the Number Line

What number goes in the box below each number line?

Number Line 1

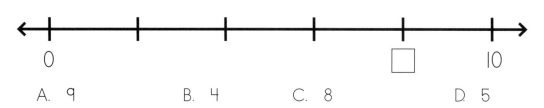

A. 9   B. 4   C. 8   D. 5

Explain your choice:

Number Line 2

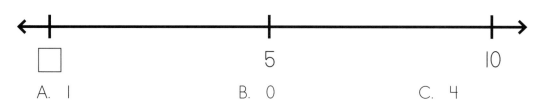

A. 1   B. 0   C. 4

Explain your choice:

Number Line 3

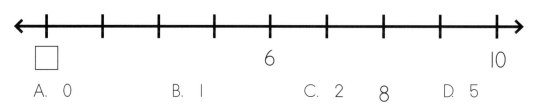

A. 0   B. 1   C. 2   8   D. 5

Explain your choice:

Teacher Notes:
Labeling the Number Line

Questions to Consider About the Key Mathematical Concepts

Are students able to locate and label points on the number line? To what extent do they

- understand that a number occupies a specific location on a number line?
- understand equal intervals on a number line?
- use information provided by labeled hash marks on a number line?

Common Core Connection (3.NF)

Grade: Third

Domain: Number and Operations—Fractions (NF)

Cluster:

A. Develop understanding of fractions as numbers.

3.NF.A.2. Understand a fraction as a number on the number line; represent fractions on a number line diagram.

Note: While not specifically mentioned in the K–2 standards, whole number work on the number line is foundational to the third grade standards, in which students use number line model for work with fractions.

Uncovering of Student Understanding About the Key Concepts

Using the Labeling the Number Line Probe can provide information about how the student is thinking about representing numbers using the number line representation.

Do they

- consider how an interval is partitioned and use the information given to determine the size of an interval?

OR

- count forwards or backwards, skip-count, or use other strategies to determine the missing label?

OR

- understand that an interval is the distance between two hash marks?

Do they

- think that the interval is always one unit?

OR

- count only from the left side of the number line to determine missing hash mark labels?

OR

- count hash marks to determine labels?

Exploring Excerpts From Educational Resources and Related Research

Common areas of difficulty for students:

In one study, students were given a number line marked only with the positions of the numbers 1 and 10 and were asked to put the numbers 0, 5, and 8 on the number line. Values the students assigned near the endpoints were generally approximately correct, but in over 95% of the pupils' work, there was no idea of proportionality when putting numbers on the line. For second graders, most of the answers given had the numbers 0, 5, and 8 all located between 1 and 5 on the line. (Littler & Jirotkova, 2008, p. 8)

Results of three experiments indicated that the more linear children's magnitude representations were, the more closely their memory of the numbers approximated the numbers presented. (Thompson & Siegler, 2010, p. 1276)

Research shows that systematic use of visual representations and manipulatives may lead to important gains in math achievement. Four studies that used visual models (one of which taught students to use number lines to understand math facts) demonstrated gains in math facts and operations. (Gersten et al., 2009, pp. 30–31)

Surveying the Prompts and Selected Responses in the Probe

This Probe contains three number line items, each with three or four possible responses and a place for students to explain their choice. The selected responses are designed to elicit common misconceptions such as counting misconceptions and overgeneralizing about what number lines should look like (start at 0 and end at 10).

The correct responses are for Number Line 1: C. 8; for Number Line 2 B. 0, and for Number Line 3: C. 2. In addition to checking for correct answers, check that explanations provide evidence of understanding of how the number line is partitioned and of the size of the intervals. If a student selects one of the incorrect answers, it is likely the student has a misconception, as described below.

Number Line 1

If a student chooses	It is likely that the student
A	• counts back one interval from 10.
B	• counts hash marks up from 0.
C	• counts all of the hash marks, even the one that is labeled 0.

Number Line 2

If a student chooses	It is likely that the student
A	• starts the number line at 1, perhaps because this is what the student is familiar with and/or the student lacks an understanding of 0.
C	• counts back one from 5.

Number Line 3

If a student chooses	It is likely that the student
A	• begins the number line at 0. This may be what the student is used to seeing on number lines.
B	• begins the number line at 1.
D	• counts back one from 6.

Teaching Implications and Considerations

Ideas for eliciting more information from students about their understanding and difficulties:

- For both students who correctly labeled the boxes and those who did not, ask questions to verify their understanding, such as the following:
  - How did you determine which number goes in the box?
  - What information on the number line did you use to help you figure out your answer?
  - Were any of the number lines easier for you than others? Why?

Ideas for planning instruction in response to what you learned from the results of administering the Probe:

- Help students to understand the connections between counting objects and counting on the number line. Give them practice counting on the number line and experience with the idea that they are counting the distance from 0 to 1, not starting at 1 as they do when they count objects.
- Encourage children to count in different directions and by different intervals (skip-counting by 2 and 5), so they gain flexibility with the idea of changing intervals.
- Create a number line with masking tape on the floor to provide children with a kinesthetic experience of "walking the number line."
- Help students understand the structure of number lines. For example, bigger numbers are always to the right of smaller numbers.

- Vary the endpoints on number lines to avoid the overgeneralization that all number lines start at 0 and go to 10.
- Have students partition blank number lines to build an understanding of equal intervals.

Sample Student Responses to Labeling the Number Line

Responses That Suggest Difficulty

Sample Student Response 1

Number Line 1

Selected Response: D

Explanation: I counted by ones.

Sample Student Response 2

Number Line 3

Selected Response: A

Explanation: Because it starts with 0.

Responses That Suggest Understanding

Sample Student Response 3

Number Line 1

Selected Response: C

Explanation: I start at 0 and skip-count up to 10, so it's 8.

Are They Equivalent?

3.4

1. Without adding the two numbers, use what you know about adding two-digit numbers to decide which of the number expressions below are equivalent to

$$23 + 45$$

	Circle One	Explain Your Answer
A. 25 + 43	Yes No	
B. 24 + 35	Yes No	
C. 32 + 54	Yes No	
D. 45 + 23	Yes No	
E. 20 + 48	Yes No	

2. Without subtracting, use what you know about subtracting two-digit numbers to decide which of the number expressions below are equivalent to

68 – 43

	Circle One	Explain Your Answer
A. 71 – 40	Yes No	
B. 70 – 45	Yes No	
C. 68 – 48 + 5	Yes No	
D. 63 – 48	Yes No	
E. 43 – 68	Yes No	

Teacher Notes: Are They Equivalent?

Questions to Consider About the Key Mathematical Concepts

Do students understand that the placement of a digit within a number determines its value, and can they apply that understanding to determining equivalent expressions in addition and subtraction? To what extent do they

- understand that they can increase the digit in the tens place of one addend and decrease the digit in the tens place of the other addend without changing the sum of the two numbers?
- understand that moving digits *within* a two- or three-digit number will, except in cases where that digit is the same, change the value of that number?
- apply an understanding of the operation of subtraction and place value to determine whether number expressions are equivalent?

Common Core Connection (2.NBT)

Grade: Second

Domain: Number and Operations in Base Ten (NBT)

Cluster:

B. Use place value understanding and properties of operations to add subtract.

2. NBT.B.7. Add and subtract within 1,000, using concrete models or drawings and strategies based on place value, properties of operations, and/or the relationship between addition and subtraction; relate the strategy to a written method. Understand that in adding or subtracting three-digit numbers, one adds or subtracts hundreds and hundreds, tens and tens, ones and ones; and sometimes it is necessary to compose or decompose tens or hundreds.

2. NBT.B.9. Explain why addition and subtraction strategies work, using place value and the properties of operations.

Uncovering Student Understanding About the Key Concepts

Using the Are They Equivalent? Probe can provide information about how the student is thinking about place value considerations for addition and subtraction of two-digit numbers.

Do they

- determine the value of a number by considering both the digits contained in a number and the placement of those digits within the number?

OR

- apply understanding of key number and operations ideas to facilitate computation, such as

  o composition and decomposition?
  o commutativity and associativity?
  o conservation of number?

Do they

- determine value of a digit strictly based on the numeral?

OR

- have limited strategies for addition and subtraction based on procedures?

Exploring Excerpts From Educational Resources and Related Research

Common areas of difficulty for students:

Even students who can count and identify numbers often have difficulty with positional knowledge and digit correspondence activities. (Hanich et al., 2001, p. 623)

"Place value is foundational to all work with whole numbers, and the lack of understanding of place value leads to most errors when computing with these numbers." (Sowder & Nickerson, 2010, p. 23)

"Flexible methods for computation require a strong understanding of the operations and properties of the operations, especially the commutative property and the associative property. How addition and subtraction are related as inverse operations is also an important ingredient.

"Flexible methods for computing, especially mental methods, allow students to reason much more effectively in every area of mathematics involving numbers." (Van de Walle et al., 2013, p. 216)

"A concerted effort over an extended period of time is required to establish appropriate notions of equality." (Falkner, Levi, & Carpenter 1999, p. 233, as quoted in Bamberger, Oberdorf, & Schulz-Farrell, 2010, p. 57)

Surveying the Prompts and Selected Responses in the Probe

This Probe contains five addition items and five subtraction items designed to elicit understandings and common difficulties as described below.

Addition Expression

If a student chooses	It is likely that the student
YES for A, D, and E (the correct answers)	• applies an understanding of place value to reason about the equality of the expressions, especially if there is no evidence of actual computation.
YES for B and C (incorrect answers)	• thinks that digits can always be switched around within a number without changing the sum. For example, they incorrectly think that a 4 in the ones place and a 4 in the tens place both have a value of 4. (See Sample Student Response 1.)
NO for A and/or D (incorrect answers)	• does not apply understanding of commutativity: ➤ A: 3 and 5 are each in the ones place, and they can be switched without changing the sum. 3 + 5 is the same as 5 + 3. ➤ D: Because addition is commutative, the order of the addends can be switched without changing the sum: 45 + 23 is the same as 23 + 45. (See Sample Student Response 1.)
NO for E (incorrect answer)	• lacks understanding of conservation of number and/or the operation of addition. Decreasing one addend by 3 (23 to 20) and increasing the other addend by 3 (45 to 48) results in the same sum.

Subtraction Expression

If a student chooses	It is likely that the student
YES on B and C (correct answers)	• applies an understanding of place value, especially if the student reasons about the numbers and the operation of subtraction without having made calculations. (See Sample Student Response 3.)
NO on B YES on A (incorrect answers)	• lacks understanding of place value and the operation of subtraction or applies addition reasoning: If you increase one addend by one, you need to decrease the other addend by one—but this does not apply with the operation of subtraction. If two numbers in a subtraction problem are increased by the same amount, the difference remains the same.
NO on C (incorrect answer)	• expects equivalent expressions to have the same number of terms. They might be unfamiliar with a three-term expression.
YES on A & D YES on E (incorrect answers)	• misapplies place value ideas for addition to subtraction. • thinks subtraction is commutative.

Teaching Implications and Considerations

Ideas for eliciting more information from students about their understanding and difficulties:

- How did you use estimation and reasoning to decide on your responses?
- In what ways are addition and subtraction alike and different?
- What does it mean for two expressions to be equivalent?
- Can you think of another expression that is equivalent to this one?

Ideas for planning instruction in response to what you learned from the results of administering the Probe:

- Ask questions that reinforce place value ideas related to the base-ten number system. (For example, What is 10 more? What is 10 less? What's 100 more? What is 100 less? If I add 10 to this number, what do I have to do to the other number to keep the sum the same?)
- Practice composing and decomposing numbers by their place value quantities. Use physical models such as base-ten blocks or straws to help build a visual model of place value and trading out.
- Combine the use of concrete models with their numeric expressions to reinforce the idea that a digit's value is determined by its location in the number.
- Use concrete materials such as straws and base-ten blocks to explore a variety of addition and subtraction problems and reflect on the differences between these operations, specifically with regard to commutativity.

Sample Student Responses to Are They Equivalent?

Responses That Suggest Difficulty

Sample Student Response 1

B. 24 + 35 is equivalent to 23 + 45 because there are two odd numbers and two even numbers.

Sample Student Response 2

E. 20 + 48 is not equivalent to 23 + 45 because you're adding two different numbers. The numbers are not equal.

Responses That Suggest Understanding

Sample Student Response 3

B. 70 − 45 is equivalent to 68 − 43

You can add 2 more to 68 you get 70 but then you take 2 more away from 43. So, it's the same.

Are They Equivalent?

1. Without adding the two numbers, use what you know about adding three-digit numbers to decide which of the number expressions below are equivalent to

$$427 + 569$$

	Circle One	Explain Your Answer
A. 724 + 965	Yes No	
B. 467 + 529	Yes No	
C. 527 + 469	Yes No	
D. 472 + 596	Yes No	
E. 927 + 69	Yes No	

2. Without subtracting, use what you know about subtracting three-digit numbers to decide which of the number expressions below are equivalent to

618 – 498

	Circle One	Explain Your Answer
A. 620 – 500	Yes No	
B. 681 – 489	Yes No	
C. 608 – 488	Yes No	
D. 698 – 418	Yes No	
E. 618 – 418 – 80	Yes No	

4

Operations and Algebraic Thinking Probes

The content of the Probes in this chapter aligns with operations and algebraic thinking for grades 1 and 2. The Probes and their variations will also be relevant for kindergarteners who have met their grade-level standards.

We developed these Probes to address the critical areas of focus in operations and algebraic thinking for grades 1 and 2, described in the standards (CCSSO, 2010) as follows.

Grade 1: Developing understanding of addition, subtraction; strategies for addition and subtraction within 20

Students

- use a variety of models to model and understand add-to, take-from, put-together, take-apart, and compare situations.
- understand connections between counting and addition and subtraction.
- use properties of addition to add whole numbers and to create and use increasingly sophisticated strategies based on these properties.
- build their understanding of the relationship between addition and subtraction.

The content of the Probes in this chapter aligns with operations and algebraic thinking for grades 1 and 2. The Probes and their variations will also be relevant for kindergarteners who have met their grade-level standards.

Grade 2: Building fluency with addition and subtraction

Students

- use their understanding of addition to develop fluency with addition and subtraction.
- solve problems by applying their understanding of models for addition and subtraction.
- develop, discuss, and use efficient, accurate, and generalizable methods to compute sums and differences of whole numbers.
- select and accurately apply methods to mentally calculate sums and differences.

The standards and their related questions, as well as the Probes associated with them, are shown in the table below.

Common Core Math Content

Common Core Mathematical Content	Related Question	Probe Name
Represent and solve problems involving addition and subtraction. Understand and apply properties of operations and the relationship between addition and subtraction. Add and subtract within 20. **1.OA.A.1, 1.OA.B.3, 1.OA.C.5**	Are students able to determine all of the ways in which two numbers can be combined by addition to give a sum of 10?	Apples and Oranges (p. 103)
Add and subtract within 20. **1.OA.C.6**	Are students able to combine two numbers to determine the sum of the numbers?	Sums of Ten (p. 109)
Work with addition and subtraction equations. **1.OA.D.7, 1.OA.D.8**	Do students apply an understanding of equality and the operation of addition to determine the missing value in an equation?	Completing Number Sentences (p. 118)
Represent and solve problems involving addition and subtraction. **2.OA.D.7, 1.OA.D.8**	When solving problems involving combining, comparing, and separating, can students make sense of the sequence of actions in the problem to determine an appropriate strategy?	Solving Number Stories (p. 123)

Apples and Oranges

Sasha is filling a bowl with apples and oranges.

I put 5 apples and 5 oranges in the bowl.

Is there another way to fill this bowl with apples and oranges and have exactly 10 pieces of fruit in it?

YES   NO

Explain your answer. Write number sentences to show your thinking.

Teacher Notes:
Apples and Oranges

Questions to Consider About the Key Mathematical Concepts

Are students able to determine all of the ways in which two numbers can be combined by addition to give a sum of 10? To what extent do they

- apply understanding of quantity, part–whole relationship, and compensation?
- represent sums of ten by writing number sentences?

Common Core Connection (1.OA)

Grade: First

Domain: Operations and Algebraic Thinking (OA)

Clusters:

A. Represent and solve problems involving addition and subtraction.

1. OA.A.1. Use addition and subtraction within 20 to solve word problems involving situations of adding to, taking from, putting together, taking apart, and comparing, with unknowns in all positions, e.g., by using objects, drawings, and equations with a symbol for the unknown number to represent the problem.

B. Understand and apply properties of operations and the relationship between addition and subtraction.

1. OA.B.3. Apply properties of operations as strategies to add and subtract. Examples: If $8 + 3 = 11$ is known, then $3 + 8 = 11$ is also known (commutative property of addition). To add $2 + 6 + 4$, the second two numbers can be added to make a ten, so $2 + 6 + 4 = 2 + 10 = 12$ (associative property of addition).

C. Add and subtract within 20.

1. OA.C.5. Relate counting to addition and subtraction (e.g., by counting on 2 to add 2).

Uncovering Student Understanding About the Key Concepts

Using the Apples and Oranges Probe can provide the following information about how students are thinking about combining numbers to make a sum of 10.

Do they

- use knowledge of addition fact families to find sums of ten?

OR

Do they

- think there is only one way to make a sum of 10?

Do they

- understand compensation—the idea that in order to maintain the quantity of a set, if I increase the quantity of one addend by one, I must decrease the quantity of the other by one?

OR

Do they

- increase one quantity without decreasing the other quantity?

- apply an understanding of the problem context—6 apples and 4 oranges is different from 4 apples and 6 oranges?

OR

- identify sums of numbers without consideration of the problem context?

Exploring Excerpts From Educational Resources and Related Research

Common areas of difficulty and development for students:

The big idea of hierarchical inclusion leads to two more big ideas: compensation and part/whole relationship. "Once children construct an understanding of hierarchical inclusion they can begin to consider compensation." (Fosnot & Dolk, 2001, p. 36)

"If 6 + 1 = 7 then necessarily 5 + 2 = 7 as well, because while one more has been removed from the six, it has been added to the one—compensation. . . . As this idea of compensation is extended to generate other ways to make 7, a deeper understanding of the relationship of parts to whole is constructed. If 5 + 2 = 7. Then 7 − 2 = 5." (Fosnot & Dolk, 2001, p. 36)

"Part-whole understanding of number provides a stronger conceptual base for addition and subtraction strategies. . . . Children in a kindergarten study transferred their part-whole knowledge to the solution of simple addition and subtraction word problems, with twice as many problems solved than by children taught to count by ones." (Jensen, 1993, p. 51)

"One of the most important reasoning strategies for basic facts is to make use of known facts to derive other basic facts. Other facts are often built on knowledge of the facts that sum to ten. Students who do not gain this skill are at a significant disadvantage when learning facts with the sums eleven through eighteen and when computing with greater numbers." (Dacey & Collins, 2010, p. A16)

Surveying the Prompts and Selected Responses in the Probe

This Probe consists of one yes/no prompt with a supporting explanation. The item is designed to elicit understandings and common difficulties as described below.

If a student chooses	It is likely that the student
No	• does not understand part–whole relationship or conservation. • does not understand the problem-solving situation given.

Yes
(correct answer)
A = apples
R = oranges
10 A + 0 R = 10
0 A + 10 R = 10
9 A + 1 R = 10
1 A + 9 R = 10
8 A + 2 R = 10
2 A + 8 R = 10
7 A + 3 R = 10
3 A + 7 R = 10
6 A + 4 R = 10
4 A + 6 R = 10
5 A + 5 R = 10
	• recognizes that there is more than one way to fill a bowl with apples and oranges to make a total of 10 items in the bowl.
	• *If the student's explanation includes all the possible number sentences, it is likely that the student*
	  o understands conservation and addition fact families.
	  o can systematically identify all of the pairs of numbers that add to 10.
	  o recognizes that 10 apples and 0 oranges, and 0 apples and 10 oranges, are also possible combinations.

Teaching Implications and Considerations

Ideas for eliciting more information from students about their understanding and difficulties:

- For students who determined there is more than one way to fill the fruit bowl, ask,
  - o How did you determine the ways that Sasha could fill the fruit bowl?
  - o How do you know that you have found all of the ways that Sasha can fill the bowl?
- If the students struggled to find multiple combinations of apples and oranges, offer a simpler example to see if they approach the task any differently:
  - o If Sasha wanted to put a total of only 5 pieces of fruit in the bowl, how many ways could she fill the bowl?

Ideas for planning instruction in response to what you learned from the results of administering the Probe:

- Provide concrete materials, such as a collection of orange counters, cubes, or tiles to represent oranges and a collection of red counters, cubes, or tiles to represent apples. Ask students to build the different combinations of apples and oranges that Sasha could put in the bowl. Physically building may help students make sense of the context and identify the combinations they have missed.

- Provide a template with two rows of 5 blocks or one row of 10 (see example below) to help students organize and record information. These can help them to see patterns that they might use to determine if they have found all of the combinations.

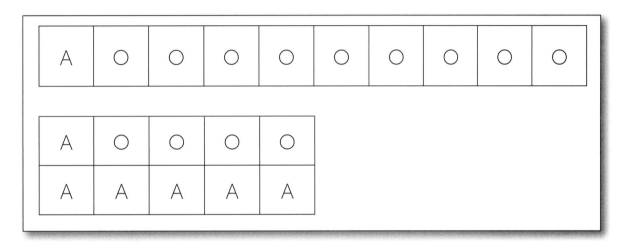

Sample Student Responses to Apples and Oranges

Responses That Suggest Difficulty

Sample Student Response 1

Student circled no and wrote, "Sasha can fill the bowl with 5 apples and 5 oranges because 5 + 5 equals 10. Or else there will not be 10."

Sample Student Response 2

Student circled yes and wrote

$$5 + 5 = 10$$

$$6 + 4 = 10$$

$$3 + 7 = 10$$

$$8 + 2 = 10$$

$$1 + 9 = 10$$

Apples and Oranges Variation

Sasha is filling a bowl with fruit.

She has some apples,   and she has some oranges.

Sasha wants to have exactly 10 pieces of fruit in the bowl.

Three students were working on this same problem.

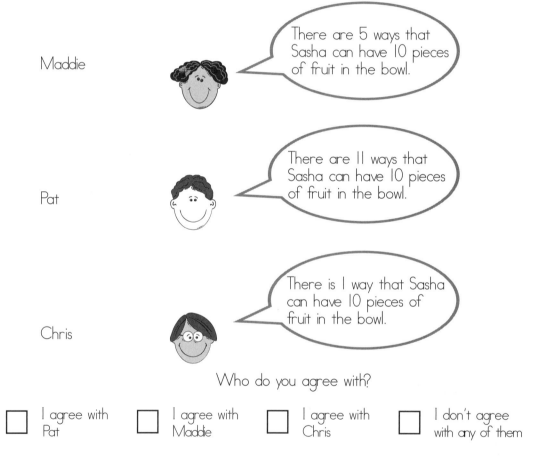

Maddie: There are 5 ways that Sasha can have 10 pieces of fruit in the bowl.

Pat: There are 11 ways that Sasha can have 10 pieces of fruit in the bowl.

Chris: There is 1 way that Sasha can have 10 pieces of fruit in the bowl.

Who do you agree with?

☐ I agree with Pat   ☐ I agree with Maddie   ☐ I agree with Chris   ☐ I don't agree with any of them

Now, write down all the number sentences that show why you agree.

Sums of Ten

(Card Sort; reproducible cards and recording sheets follow Teacher Notes on p. 114)

Ten	NOT Ten
8 + 2	3 + 7
6 + 4	4 + ::
I + ::::	2 + 7 + I
:::: + ::	7 + 5

5 + 5	2 + 6 + 3
5 + I + 4	:: + 8
::: + ::::	9 + I
10 + 0	3 + 4 + 4

Advance Preparation: Create cards by photocopying the reproducible on p. 114 on card stock and cutting the cards apart along the lines. Separate the two blank cards and the two label cards from the deck, and shuffle the rest of the cards.

Instructions: Invite the student(s) to sort the cards into 2 piles: **Ten** and **NOT Ten**. Use the label cards to identify the piles.

As students finish the sort, give them the blank cards, and ask them to create their own **Ten** and **NOT Ten** cards.

Ask students to choose three cards from the **Ten** pile (or choose three cards for them). Ask them to explain or show how they knew these cards should go in the **Ten** pile.

Ask students to choose three cards from the **NOT Ten** pile (or choose three cards for them). Ask them to explain or show how they knew these cards should go in the **NOT Ten** pile. Use the recording sheet as appropriate.

Teacher Notes: Sums of Ten

Questions to Consider About the Key Mathematical Concepts

Are students able to combine two numbers to determine the sum of the numbers? To what extent do they

- determine whether two or more numbers, given in numeric or image form, combine to a given third number?
- use a range of strategies, including count-all, count-on, known facts, and composing or decomposing numbers, into known facts?

Common Core Connection (1.OA)

Grade: First

Domain: Operations and Algebraic Thinking (OA)

Cluster:

C. Add and subtract within 20.

1. OA.C.1. Add and subtract within 20, demonstrating fluency for addition and subtraction within 10. Use strategies such as counting on; making ten (e.g., $8 + 6 = 8 + 2 + 4 = 10 + 4 = 14$); decomposing a number leading to a ten (e.g., $13 - 4 = 13 - 3 - 1 = 10 - 1 = 9$); using the relationship between addition and subtraction (e.g., knowing that $8 + 4 = 12$, one knows $12 - 8 = 4$); and creating equivalent but easier or known sums (e.g., adding $6 + 7$ by creating the known equivalent $6 + 6 + 1 = 12 + 1 = 13$).

Uncovering Student Understanding About the Key Concepts

Using the Sums of Ten Probe can provide the following information about how the students are thinking about determining the sum of two or three numbers.

Do they

- determine the sum by
  - counting on from a given number?
  - subitizing and combining quantities?
  - using addition fact families?
- use addition fact families when finding both sums of ten and sums that are not ten?

OR

Do they

- count all starting at 1 each time?

OR

- use addition fact families only when the numbers have a sum of ten?

Do they

- start with the larger number when   OR
  counting on?

- determine the sum when given a   OR
  number in numeric form without
  having to draw it?

Do they

- start with the first
  number given?

- use or draw objects in
  order to determine the
  sum?

Note: Use of an efficient strategy for this Probe is dependent upon the prior experiences of students. Because of this, the goal for giving the task may change. These Teacher Notes focus on strategy development with an expectation that students have had enough experience in the classroom with building sums of tens with objects, modeling addition problems with a variety of contexts, counting all to find totals, and subitizing. Therefore the research and considerations will focus on strategies beyond count-all.

Exploring Excerpts From Educational Resources and Related Research

Common areas of difficulty for students:

"Learning Pitfall . . . Students may continue counting every object instead of taking advantage of knowing one quantity and then counting on from that number to find a sum." (Bay Area Mathematics Task Force, 1999, p. 16)

"Although some educators once believed that children memorize their 'basic facts' as conditioned responses, research shows that children do not move from knowing nothing about the sums and differences of numbers to having the basic number combinations memorized. Instead, they move through a series of progressively more advanced and abstract methods for working out the answers to simple arithmetic problems. Most children continue to use those procedures occasionally and for some computations. Recall eventually becomes the predominant method for some children, but current research methods cannot adequately distinguish between answers produced by recall and those generated by fast (nonrecall) procedures." (National Research Council, 2005, pp. 182–183)

"During the early childhood years, their understanding of number is fragile, and learning to count on is not an all-or-nothing proposition. Teachers may see children counting on with small collections and find that this strategy is not yet generalized to larger collections. Children may count on using one concrete material but not others. The context also may determine whether a child uses the counting-on strategy. Sometimes, a child will count on in one activity and then, in the next activity, need to count one by one from the beginning to confirm the number." (Weiland, 2007, p. 191)

"Counting on is a very difficult strategy for children to construct, because they almost have to negate their earlier strategy of counting from the beginning. Understanding why the strategy works depends on developing a sense of cardinality [the number of objects in a set] and hierarchical inclusion [numbers build by exactly one each time and are nested within each other by this amount]." Without understanding part/whole relationships and compensation, children often make no connection between similar problems (for example, two problems both requiring students to add 7 and 3). Instead, they solve it by counting again each time. (Fosnot & Dolk, 2001, pp. 36–37)

Surveying the Prompts and Selected Responses in the Probe

There are 18 cards: 10 cards with sums of **Ten** and 8 cards with sums that are **NOT Ten**. The prompts and selected responses are designed to elicit understandings and common difficulties as described below:

If a student	It is likely that the student did one or more of the following:
excludes a Ten card	• incorrect subitizing when given dot figures. (See Sample Student Response 1.) • incorrect counting on by counting the number name twice, for example, counting 6, 7, 8, 9 for 6 + 4 rather than counting on from the 6 as 7, 8, 9, 10. (See Sample Student Response 2.)
includes a Not Ten card	• incorrect subitizing when given dot figures. • using "known facts" incorrectly. • using three addends incorrectly. (See Sample Student Response 3.)

Teaching Implications and Considerations

Ideas for eliciting more information from students about their understanding and difficulties:

- When choosing the cards to ask for an explanation, consider the level of understanding of the individual student. Some examples:
  - For students who are still counting all, choose cards that use a number and a dot image, as these are more likely to cause students to count on.
  - For students who have developed a recall of "known facts," choose cards in which further processing is necessary (such as the cards with three addends).
- For those who exclude one or more **Ten** cards, be sure to include the card or cards when choosing three cards to ask for follow-up explanations.

- For those who include one or more **NOT Ten** cards, be sure to include the card or cards when choosing three cards to ask for follow-up explanations.

Ideas for planning instruction in response to what you learned from the results of administering the Probe:

- Provide multiple opportunities requiring conceptual subitizing.
- Prior to asking students to solve combinations devoid of a context, provide multiple opportunities for students to directly model story problems requiring addition, and to share their different strategies for modeling the addition operation.
- To build understanding of compensation, a skill needed for understanding counting on as a strategy, use "cover-up" activities, where a number of counters are hidden and more are added.
- Once students have demonstrated an understanding of the meaning of combining, have already shown efficiency with counting on, and have moved on to be able to recall "known facts"; only occasionally require students to explain why they know the sum of a given number expression. Doing so too often may cause students to think they should always revert back to a counting strategy.

Sample Student Responses to Sums of Ten

Responses That Suggest Difficulty

Sample Student Response 1: $\boxed{\begin{smallmatrix} \bullet\bullet\bullet \\ \bullet\bullet \end{smallmatrix} + 4}$ There are 5 dots and 4 more so it is missing 1.

Sample Student Response 2: $\boxed{3 + 7}$ Student counts on from 3 and uses fingers to count on 7 but misses a finger and lands on 9 rather than 10.

Sample Student Response 3: $\boxed{2 + 6 + 3}$ Student adds 6 and 2 to get 8 but then forgets to add on the 3.

Cards for Sums of Ten

Ten	Not Ten
8 + 2	3 Regular 7
6 + 4	4 + ∷∷
1 + ⦂⦂⦂	2 + 7 + 1
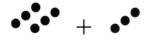 + ⦂⦂	7 + 5

4.2a

$5 + 5$	$2 + 6 + 3$
$5 + 1 + 4$	•• $+ 8$
••• $+$ ••••	$9 + 1$
$10 + 0$	$3 + 4 + 4$

Recording Sheet

TEN

Card 1 (Tape card to sheet or draw it.)	Show Why
Card 2 (Tape card to sheet or draw it.)	Show Why
Card 3 (Tape card to sheet or draw it.)	Show Why

Recording Sheet
NOT Ten

Card 1 (Tape card to sheet or draw it.)	Show Why
Card 2 (Tape card to sheet or draw it.)	Show Why
Card 3 (Tape card to sheet or draw it.)	Show Why

Completing Number Sentences

4.3

I. $3 + 3 = \boxed{} + 5$ Circle the number that belongs in the box: 6 11 1	Write about how you got your answer.
2. $8 + 3 = 7 + \boxed{}$ Circle the number that belongs in the box: 11 4 18	Write about how you got your answer.
3. $6 + \boxed{} = 8 + 7$ Circle the number that belongs in the box: 21 9 2	Write about how you got your answer.
4. $3 + 5 = \boxed{} + 4$ Circle the number that belongs in the box: 4 8 12	Write about how you got your answer.

Teacher Notes: Completing Number Sentences

Questions to Consider About the Key Mathematical Concepts

Do students apply an understanding of equality and the operation of addition to determine the missing value in an equation? To what extent do they

- think flexibly about equations and the meaning of the equal sign?
- demonstrate an understanding of the operation of addition and foundational number concepts related to addition?

Common Core Connection (1.OA)

Grade: First

Domain: Operations and Algebraic Thinking (OA)

Cluster:

D. Work with addition and subtraction equations.

1. OA.D.7. Understand the meaning of the equal sign, and determine if equations involving addition and subtraction are true or false. For example, which of the following equations are true, and which are false? $6 = 6$, $7 = 8 - 1$, $5 + 2 = 2 + 5$, $4 + 1 = 5 + 2$.

1. OA.D.8. Determine the unknown whole number in an addition or subtraction equation relating three whole numbers. For example, determine the unknown number that makes the equation true in each of the equations $8 + ? = 11$, $5 = \underline{\hspace{1cm}} - 3$, $6 + 6 = \underline{\hspace{1cm}}$.

Uncovering Student Understanding About the Key Concepts

Using the Completing Number Sentences Probe can provide information about how students are thinking about equality and the meaning of the equal sign.

Do they

- correctly interpret aspects of the equation, such as
  - the addends?
  - the equal sign?
  - the box symbol representing the missing value?

OR

Do they

- add quantities without consideration of all of the numbers and symbols contained in the equation?

Do they

- apply an understanding of the equal sign as a symbol of equality that tells them the quantities on each side have the same value?

- apply number concepts such as hierarchical inclusion, compensation, decomposition, and composition to determine the missing value?

OR

OR

Do they

- interpret the equal sign as a sort of stop sign that means "when you reach the equal sign, it's time to compute"?

- rely only on counting or counting on to determine a sum?

Note: Have concrete materials such as counters or cubes available to students should they request them to assist them in their problem solving. If students seem to have some knowledge of the tasks but are struggling or frustrated with the computation, consider offering these, but do not offer them from the start.

Exploring Excerpts From Educational Resources and Related Research

Common areas of difficulty for students:

"In grades K–2, equality is an important algebraic concept that students must encounter and begin to understand. A common explanation for the equal sign given by students is that 'the answer is coming,' but they need to recognize that the equals sign indicates a relationship—that the quantities on each side are equivalent." (NCTM, 2000, p. 94)

"The equal sign is one of the most important symbols in elementary arithmetic, in algebra, add all mathematics using numbers and operations. At the same time research dating from 1975 to the present indicates that '=' is a very poorly understood symbol. . . . Students' experiences lead them to believe that one side of the equal sign—usually the left side—is the problem and the other side is the answer. Their understanding of = is more like the button on the calculator—it is what you press to get the answer. It separates the problem from the answer." (Van de Walle, 2007, p. 260)

"Knowing different methods of computation will be of little value to students if they do not understand what each operation does. As our students solve problems in the world around them, they must understand the *meaning* of each operation if they are to know which operations to compute and which numbers to use within a problem situation. . . . Without such 'deep meanings' for the operations, students tend to merely react to the symbols they see and do not make the needed connections conceptually. For example, the student who sees $56 + \square = 83$ may think '56 and 83'; it is *plus* so you add the numbers." (Ashlock, 2006, pp. 53–54)

Surveying the Prompts and Selected Responses in the Probe

There are four number sentences, each with two terms on each side of the equal sign and one missing value. The items are designed to elicit understandings and common difficulties as described below.

If a student chooses	It is likely that the student
6 on #1 11 on #2 2 on #3 8 on #4	• attends to only two of the terms in the equation along with the missing number box, ignoring the third term and demonstrating lack of understanding of the structure of the equation and/or the meaning of the equal sign.
11 on #1 18 on #2 21 on #3 12 on #4	• has added all of the numbers shown in the equation, disregarding the structure of the equation, the location of the unknown box, and the meaning and location of the equal sign.
1 on #1 4 on #2 9 on #3 4 on #4	• understands the structure of the equation and the meaning of the equal sign as a symbol of equivalence, and is able to apply addition facts to solve the problem. Look for indication of the student's understanding in the written explanations of how the student got the answer. (See Sample Student Response 1.)

Teaching Implications and Considerations

Ideas for eliciting more information from students about their understanding and difficulties:

- For students who appear to treat the equal sign as a signal to stop and compute, ask some questions directed at learning more about their understanding of the equal sign and equations:
  - What does the equal sign mean to you? (Is the student thinking about the equal sign only as "the answer is coming"?)
  - What does this blank box in the equation mean to you?
  - Can you read this equation out loud to me?
  - How does this equation look the same or different from others that you have seen?
- To learn about how the student approached answer the problems, ask:
  - What did you do to decide on an answer choice?
  - Can you build this equation using concrete objects?

Ideas for planning instruction in response to what you learned from the results of administering the Probe:

- During instruction, use explicit language, such as "is the same as" and "is equivalent to," to refer to the equal sign as a relationship between the two numbers and/or expressions on opposite sides of the symbol.
- Connect and contrast the equal sign to symbols of inequality to build understanding of equality.
- Use visual models that support the idea of equivalence (e.g., balance, seesaw).
- Provide opportunities for students to make connections from symbolic notation to the representation of an equation.
- Vary the way that you show addition and subtraction equations, using different numbers of terms on each side of the equal sign to avoid students developing only one image of what an equation should look like.
- Explore equations as either true or false to build understanding of the equal sign (e.g., "is this equation true or false: $8 + 7 = 5 + 9$?"), and ask students to explain their reasoning.
- Use interactive technology to have students model equivalence.

Sample Student Responses to Completing Number Sentences

Responses That Suggest Difficulty

Sample Student Response 1

$3 + 3 = \_\_ + 5$

Student chose 6 and explained: $3 + 3 = 6$ and that's what I think is right.

Sample Student Response 2

$6 + \_\_ = 8 + 7$

Student chose 21 and explained: $6 + 8$ is 14. $14 + 7 = 21$.

Responses That Suggest Understanding

Sample Student Response 3

$8 + 3 = 7 + \_\_$

Student chose 4 and explained: $8 + 3$ is equal to 11 and $7 + 4$ equals 11.

Sample Student Response 4

$3 + 3 = \_\_ + 5$

Student chose 1 and explained: I knew $3 + 3 = 6$ so I had to find $5 +$ what $=$ six.

Solving Number Stories

4.4

1. Three students each solved the following problem.

Mike has 23 toy cars. Susan has 31 toy cars. How many more toy cars does Susan have than Mike?

I think the answer is 54

Lamar

I think the answer is 8

Fran

I don't think the answer is 54 or 8

Tom

Circle the name of the student you agree with. Use words or pictures to show your thinking.

2. Three students each solved the following problem.

Paula has some grapes. Carlos gave her 18 more grapes. Now Paula has 34 grapes. How many grapes did Paula have to start with?

I think the answer is 52

Stefan

I think the answer is 16

Tasha

I don't think the answer is 52 or 16

Emma

Circle the name of the student you agree with. Use words or pictures to show your thinking.

Teacher Notes: Solving Number Stories

Questions to Consider About the Key Mathematical Concepts

When solving problems involving combining, comparing, and separating, can students make sense of the sequence of actions in the problem to determine an appropriate strategy? To what extent do they

- make sense of the sequence of actions within a problem context to determine whether to add or subtract the given numbers?
- model the situation with a number sentence or an equation that matches their solution process?
- describe how their model and solution relate back to the context?

Common Core Connection (2.OA)

Grade: Second

Domain: Operations and Algebraic Thinking (OA)

Cluster:

A. Represent and solve problems involving addition and subtraction.

    2. OA.A.1. Use addition and subtraction within 100 to solve one- and two-step word problems involving situations of adding to, taking from, putting together, taking apart, and comparing, with unknowns in all positions, e.g., by using drawings and equations with a symbol for the unknown number to represent the problem.

Uncovering Student Understanding About the Key Concepts

Using the Solving Number Stories Probe can provide the following information about how the students are thinking about comparing and joining problem types.

Do they		*Do they*
• recognize compare problems in which the difference between the two numbers is wanted?	OR	• combine the numbers to solve the problem?
• recognize join problems with the starting number unknown?	OR	• combine the numbers to solve the problem?

Do they

- find the difference using a subtraction strategy (such as count on, count back, or modeling by comparing and counting the difference)?

OR

Do they

- have difficulty subtracting the numbers?

Exploring Excerpts From Educational Resources and Related Research

Common areas of difficulty for students:

Some problem types are more difficult than others. The join or separate problems in which the start part is unknown are often the most difficult, most likely because students who tend to model problems directly do not know how many counters to begin with to model the problem. (Van de Walle, Karp, & Bay-Williams, 2013, p. 151)

The language of comparisons is difficult. Many students "hear" the part of the sentence about who has more, but do not initially hear the part about how many more; they need experience hearing and saying a separate sentence for each of the two parts in order to comprehend and say the one-sentence form. (Common Core Standards Writing Team, 2011d, p. 12)

Surveying the Prompts and Selected Responses in the Probe

The Probe consists of two problem types: one compare and one join with start unknown. The prompts and selected responses are designed to elicit understandings and common difficulties as described below:

Problem Set 1

If a student chooses	*It is likely that the student*
Lamar	• views "how many more" as a prompt for addition, and is likely to choose 54. (See Sample Student Response 1.)
Fran (correct answer)	• recognizes the context as a compare situation and successfully subtracts one number from the other.
Tom	• typically either ○ recognizes the compare situation but uses an incorrect subtraction strategy, or ○ views the "how many more" as a prompt for addition and uses an incorrect addition strategy.

Problem Set 2

If a student chooses	*It is likely that the student*
Stefan	• views "gave her more" as a prompt for addition, and is likely to choose 52. (See Sample Student Response 2.)
Tasha (correct answer)	• recognizes the context as a join problem with an unknown starting number and successfully subtracts one number from the other.

Emma	• typically either
	  ○ recognizes the join situation but uses an incorrect subtraction strategy to find the starting number (see Sample Student Response 2), or
	  ○ views "gave her more" as a prompt for addition and uses an incorrect addition strategy. (See Sample Student Response 3.)

Teaching Implications and Considerations

Ideas for eliciting more information from students about their understanding and difficulties:

- For those who choose Lamar in Problem Set 1 and/or Stefan in Problem Set 2, determine whether students are able to describe the problem's context in their own words. If they are able to do so, provide an opportunity to re-examine the choices.
- For those who choose Fran in Problem Set 1 and/or Tasha in Problem Set 2 but who do not describe or show a way of thinking about the problem as subtraction, ask,

   ○ How did you determine that Fran/Tasha has the correct answer?

- For those who choose Tom and/or Emma, the follow-up question should be determined depending on the difficulty the student showed.

Ideas for planning instruction in response to what you learned from the results of administering the Probe:

- "In developing meaning of operations, teachers should ensure that students repeatedly encounter situations in which the same numbers appear in different contexts" (NCTM, 2000, p. 83).
- Expose students multiple times to all problem types; do not focus on only those that are easier for students to solve (Van de Walle et al., 2013, p. 151).

- When the teacher models representations of number sentences, these representations should reflect the variability students show (e.g., not all students represent a compare situation as a subtraction problem). In all mathematical problem solving, what matters is the explanation a student gives to relate a representation to a context, and not the representation separated from its context (Common Core Standards Writing Team, 2011d, p. 12).

Sample Student Responses to Solving Number Stories

Responses That Suggest Difficulty

Sample Student Response 1: The answer is 54. Just add the numbers like Lamar did.

Sample Student Response 2: The answer is 24. I did 18 − 34. 8 − 4 is 4 and 3 − 1 is 2.

Sample Student Response 3: The answer is 42. I added. (Student shows 18 and 34 as 42, forgetting to add another group of 10.)

Responses That Suggest Understanding

Sample Student Response 4:

Mike has 23 ‖‖‖. ‖‖‖. ‖‖‖. ‖‖‖.|||

Susan has 31 ‖‖‖. ‖‖‖. ‖‖‖. ‖‖‖. ‖‖‖. ‖‖‖.|

Find the difference.

5

Measurement and Data Probes

The content of the Probes in this chapter aligns with the measurement and data standards for grades 1 and 2. The Probes and their variations will also be relevant for kindergarteners who have met their grade-level standards.

We developed these Probes to address the critical areas of focus in measurement and data for grades 1 and 2, described in the standards (CCSSO, 2010) as follows.

Grade 1: Developing understanding of linear measurement and measuring lengths as iterating length units

- Students develop an understanding of the meaning and processes of measurement, including underlying concepts such as iterating (the mental activity of building up the length of an object with equal-size units) and the transitivity principle for indirect measurement.

Grade 2: Using standard units of measure

The content of the Probes in this chapter aligns with the measurement and data standards for grades 1 and 2. The Probes and their variations will also be relevant for kindergarteners who have met their grade-level standards.

- Students recognize the need for standard units of measure (centimeter and inch).
- They use rulers and other measurement tools with the understanding that linear measure involves an iteration of units.
- They recognize that the smaller the unit, the more iterations they need to cover a given length.

The standards and their related questions, as well as the Probes associated with them, are shown in the table below.

Common Core Math Content

Common Core Mathematical Content	Related Question	Probe Name
Measure lengths indirectly and by iterating length units. **1.MD.A.2**	Do students understand that the length measurement of an object is the number of same-size length units that span the object with no gaps or overlaps?	Length of Rope (p. 130)
Measure and estimate lengths in standard units. **2.MD.A.2**	Do students understand the inverse relationship between the size of the unit and the number of units needed to measure an object's length?	Comparing Measures (p. 137)
Represent and interpret data. **2.MD.D.9**	Are students able to interpret the information represented in line plots in order to answer questions about the data?	Reading Line Plots (p. 143)

This chapter also includes one variation probe that addresses measurement content and provides an extension to the original probe Comparing Measures. You'll find the variation Probes after the Teacher Notes and reproducibles for the original probe.

Length of Rope

Susie is using minicrayons to measure different-size pieces of rope. The pieces of rope and minicrayons are shown below.

Problems 1–3

Decide if each piece of Susie's rope is 3 minicrayons long.	Circle One
1	Yes No
2	Yes No
3	Yes No

Explain how you decided whether to circle Yes or No:

Problems 4–6

Decide if each piece of Susie's rope is 3 minicrayons long.	Circle One
4	Yes No
5	Yes No
6	Yes No

Explain how you decided whether to circle Yes or No:

Teacher Notes:
Length of Rope

Questions to Consider About the Key Mathematical Concepts

Do students understand that the length measurement of an object is the number of same-size length units that span the object with no gaps or overlaps? To what extent do they

- understand that length can be measured by unit iteration or unit tiling?
- when iterating, move the identified unit along the length of the object to be measured without gaps or overlaps and determine the measure as the count of the number of times the unit is moved?
- when tiling, "fill" the length of the object with a collection of equal-size units without gaps or overlaps and determine the measure as the number of equal-size units needed to span the length of the object?

Common Core Connection (1.MD)

Grade: First

Domain: Measurement and Data (MD)

Cluster:

A. Measure lengths indirectly and by iterating length units.

1.MD.A.2. Express the length of an object as a whole number of length units, by laying multiple copies of a shorter object (the length unit) end to end; understand that the length measurement of an object is the number of same-size length units that span it with no gaps or overlaps. *Limit to contexts where the object being measured is spanned by a whole number of length units with no gaps or overlaps.*

Uncovering Student Understanding About the Key Concepts

Using the Length of Rope Probe can provide the following information about how the students are thinking about tiling.

Do they

- determine whether or not there are gaps in the iteration and how a gap impacts the length?

- notice any overlaps in the iteration of the unit?

OR

Do they

- ignore gaps and count the number of units to determine the measure?

OR

- ignore overlaps and count the number of units and/or partial units to determine the measure?

Do they		*Do they*
• determine if the unit is used in the same way (same length) each time?	OR	• ignore overlays and count the number of units and/or partial units to determine the measure?

Variation 5.1V is the same Probe available as a set of sortable cards allowing students to view one item at a time.

Exploring Excerpts From Educational Resources and Related Research

Common areas of difficulty for students:

"Unfortunately, measurement is an often neglected Content Standard in early childhood classrooms. Continuing debates over such topics as the ability of young children to conserve length, volume, or area; the use of standard or nonstandard tools for measuring; and the readiness of young children to measure often mean that teachers postpone the teaching of measurement until later grades or relegate it to a unit at the end of the year." (Copley et al., 2004, p. 314)

"If a typical group of first graders attempts to measure the length of their classroom by laying strips 1 meter long end to end, the strips sometimes overlap and the line can weave in a snakelike fashion." They most likely understand that they are counting the number of strips from end to end rather than the attribute (length) of the floor using a unit (the meter stick). (Van de Walle, Karp, & Bay-Williams, 2013, p. 376)

"Young children know early that properties such as length exist, but they do not initially know how to reason about these attributes or to measure them accurately. When there are no perceptually conflicting cues, preschoolers can accurately compare objects directly." (Clements & Sarama, 2007, p. 520)

Many students initially find it necessary to iterate the unit until it "fills up" the length of the object and will not extend the unit past the endpoint of the object they are measuring. (Stephan, Bowers, Cobb, & Gravemeijer, as cited in Clements & Sarama, 2007, p. 521)

Surveying the Prompts and Selected Responses in the Probe

There are three items per page for a total of six items. The prompts and selected responses are designed to elicit understandings and common difficulties as described below.

If a student chooses	It is likely that the student
(1) Yes, (2) No, (3) No, (4) No, (5) No, (6) Yes (correct answers)	• is focusing on tiling of the unit (minicrayon), and noting gaps, overlaps, and changes in size of the unit.
No on Problem 1	• has a rigid notion of tiling and the length of the unit. Instead of focusing on length, the student focuses on orientation, even though this orientation does not change the length of the unit.
Yes on Problem 2	• is not focusing on the "overlap" or may not notice the difference in the length of the minicrayons. The student is instead focusing on whether the end of the third crayon lines up with the end of the rope. (See Sample Student Response 1.)
Yes on Problem 3	• does not notice that the beginning of the rope is not lined up with the start of the first crayon. The student is instead focusing on whether the end of the third crayon lines up with the end of the rope. (See Sample Student Response 2.)
Yes on Problem 4	• counts the 3 crayons and is not focusing on the change in orientation of the unit that changes its length.
Yes on Problem 5	• counts the 3 crayons and is not focusing on the gaps in between.
No on Problem 6	• counts only 2 crayons and does not iterate to determine if the missing space is the length of a crayon. (See Sample Student Response 3.)

Teaching Implications and Considerations

Ideas for eliciting more information from students about their understanding and difficulties:

- In advance, prepare three cutouts of minicrayons for students to use to physically measure the rope if they are having difficulty. Ask the students to use the minicrayons to determine the length of the rope.
- If the actual length is different from the answer they provided, draw their attention to the discrepancy and ask, How does this compare to your answer?

Ideas for planning instruction in response to what you learned from the results of administering the Probe:

- When measuring, students should be asked to consider (1) the consequences of gaps and (2) the need for the units to lie on the path being measured (i.e., the straight line across the page) (Dietiker, Gonulates, & Smith, 2011, p. 255).

- Provide opportunities for students to determine the attribute to be measured, *and* ask them to measure a specific attribute.
- Emphasize solving problems that require measurement. Embed within those problems the need to develop a standard or same-size unit to measure with.
- Provide experiences in which students need to determine measures at various starting points on a ruler, and vary the rulers they are using.
- "Teachers should guide students' experiences by making the resources for measuring available, planning opportunities to measure, and encouraging students to explain the results of their actions. Discourse builds students' conceptual and procedural knowledge of measurement and gives teachers valuable information for reporting progress and planning next steps. The same conversations and questions that help students build vocabulary help teachers learn about students' understandings and misconceptions" (NCTM, 2000, p. 103).

Sample Student Responses to Length of Rope

Responses That Suggest Difficulty

Sample Student Response 1: Problem 2: Yes. There are three crayons so it is 3 long.

Sample Student Response 2: Problem 3: Yes. It lines up right here (points to end of rope and end of third crayon).

Sample Student Response 3: Problem 6: No. It has an empty space.

Responses That Suggest Understanding

Sample Student Response 4: On all of them I looked for 3 full crayons. It should not have space here either (points to gaps in Problem 5).

Length of Rope Cards

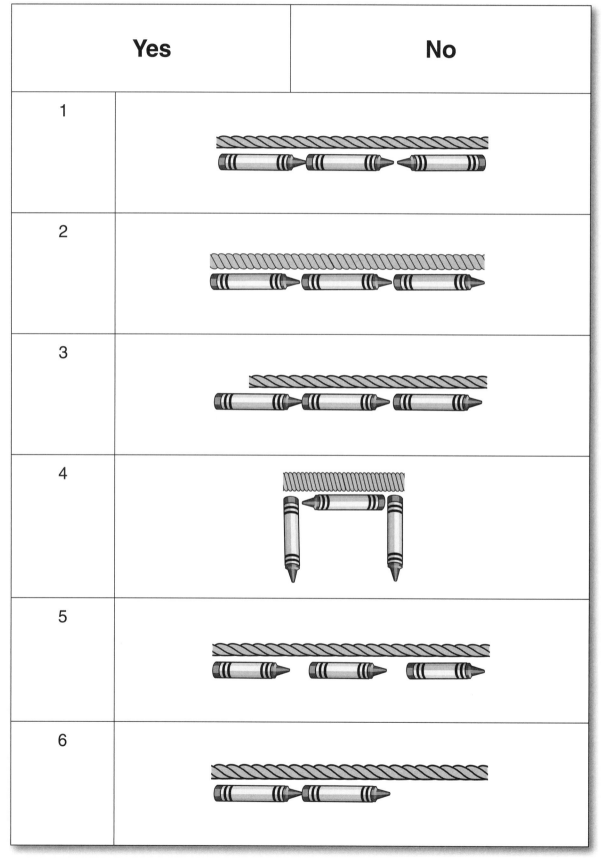

	Yes	No
1		
2		
3		
4		
5		
6		

Comparing Measures

Two students were asked to measure the length of a book using either an eraser or a paperclip. The picture shows how these items compare in size.

Kyra and Toby both measured the same book using one of the items from the picture above.

If both of them are correct, what items did they measure with?

Circle One

Kyra: eraser paperclip

Circle One

Toby: eraser paperclip

Explain your choices.

Teacher Notes: Comparing Measures

Questions to Consider About the Key Mathematical Concepts

Do students understand the inverse relationship between the size of the unit and the number of units needed to measure an object's length? To what extent do they

- understand that to span an object's length, smaller same-size units require more iterations than larger same-size units?

Common Core Connection (2.MD)

Grade: Second

Domain: Measurement and Data (MD)

Cluster:

A. Measure and estimate lengths in standard units.

2.MD.A.2. Measure the length of an object twice, using length units of different lengths for the two measurements; describe how the two measurements relate to the size of the unit chosen.

Uncovering Student Understanding About the Key Concepts

Do they

- know that the smaller the unit, the more iterations (larger number of units in the measure), and the larger the unit, the fewer iterations (smaller number of units in the measure)?

OR

- look at the relationship between the sizes of the units?

Do they

- associate the larger unit with the larger number of units in the measure and/or the smaller unit with the smaller number of units in the measure?

OR

- use the counts of the number of units to determine the answer?

Variation 5.2Va, Comparing Measures 2, elicits whether students think about the size of the unit rather than looking at the number of units when comparing two measures.

Variation 5.2Vb, Comparing Measures 3, is a more challenging variation that includes additional objects as possible units and uses 7 and 14 as the measures.

Exploring Excerpts From Educational Resources and Related Research

Common areas of difficulty for students:

"Most 7 year olds can use the concept of a unit to make inference about the relative size of objects; for example, if the numbers of units are the same but the units are different, the total size is different (Nunes and Bryant, 1996). However, they still found tasks demanding conversions of units difficult." (Clements & Sarama, 2007, p. 520)

When comparing measures of their heights, "Children easily believed that the second set of smaller bears accurately measured a rather amazing growth. When the third set of bears produced a much smaller number and one that they did not like, however, most children ignored the result. This beginning activity provided an initial experience and an impetus for the expectation to measure with multiple copies of units of the same size." (Copley et al., 2004, p. 317)

"Students, especially if they lack explicit experience with continuous attributes, may make their initial measurement judgments based upon experiences counting discrete objects. For example, researchers showed children two rows of matches. The matches in each row were of different lengths, but there was a different number of matches in each so that the rows were the same length. Although, from the adult perspective, the lengths of the rows were the same, many children argued that the row with 6 matches was longer because it had more matches. They counted units (matches), assigning a number to a *discrete* attribute (cardinality). In measuring *continuous* attributes, the sizes of the units must be considered." (Common Core Standards Writing Team, 2012a, p. 9)

Surveying the Prompts and Selected Responses in the Probe

If a student chooses	It is likely that the student
Kyra—paperclip Toby—eraser (correct choices)	understands the longer unit will result in a smaller count of the unit in the measure, and the doubling relationship of the pencil and paperclip.
Kyra—eraser Toby—paperclip	associates the count of 4 in the measure with the number of items in the picture, and doesn't consider the size of the units. (See Sample Student Response 1.)

Teaching Implications and Considerations

Ideas for eliciting more information from students about their understanding and difficulties:

- Be prepared with an eraser and paperclip. (The sizes of these do not need to have the same relationship as the sizes of the same items shown in the Probe.) Have the student measure the length of a piece of paper with two of the objects. Ask whether there were more units in the count with the longer object or the shorter object.

Ideas for planning instruction in response to what you learned from the results of administering the Probe:

- Provide opportunities for students to measure the same object with a number of different-size units.
- Using these measures, make inferences about the sizes of the units as well as the sizes of the objects.
- Second grade "is the time that measuring and reflecting on measuring the same object with different units, both standard and nonstandard, is likely to be most productive. Results of measuring with different nonstandard length-units can be explicitly compared. Students also can use the concept of unit to make inferences about the relative sizes of objects; for example, if object A is 10 regular paperclips long and object B is 10 jumbo paperclips long, the number of units is the same, but the units have different sizes, so the lengths of A and B are different" (Common Core Standards Writing Team, 2012a, pp. 13–14).

Sample Student Responses to Comparing Measures

Responses That Suggest Difficulty

Sample Student Response 1: Kyra got 4 and there are 4 erasers.

Responses That Suggest Understanding

Sample Student Response 2: You need more erasers so Toby had to use the erasers. They are smaller.

Comparing Measures 2

Circle One			Explain Your Choice
12 inches	More than Less than Same as	1 foot	
12 hours	More than Less than Same as	2 days	
2 meters	More than Less than Same as	10 centimeters	
6 days	More than Less than Same as	1 week	

Comparing Measures 3

Two students were asked to measure the length of a desk using either an eraser a pencil, a thumbtack, or a paperclip. The picture shows how these items compare in size.

Kyra and Toby both measured the same desk using one of the items from the picture above.

If both of them are correct, what items did they measure with?

	Circle One			
Kyra:	eraser	pencil	thumbtack	paperclip
	Circle One			
Toby:	eraser	pencil	thumbtack	paperclip

Explain your choices.

Reading Line Plots: Temperature

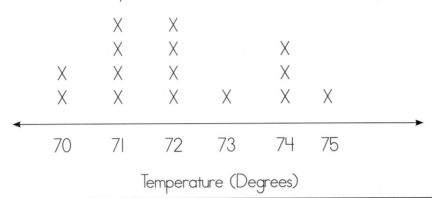

Mr. Smith's students recorded the temperature of their classroom at 2:00 each day. The line plot shows the temperatures they have recorded so far.

Temperature (Degrees)

Decide if each of the following statements about the data are true or false.

1. The temperature was 75 degrees on only 1 of the days.	True	False
Explain why:		

2. On 5 days, the temperature was 73 degrees or higher.	True	False
Explain why:		

3. The number of days at 72 degrees is 2 greater than the number of days at 74 degrees.	True	False
Explain why:		

Teacher Notes: Reading Line Plots

Questions To Consider About the Key Mathematical Concepts

Are students able to interpret the information represented in line plots in order to answer questions about the data? To what extent do they

- understand that the numbers on the scale indicate the range of values within a set of data?
- understand that each separate piece of data is shown as a dot or X over the position corresponding to the value?

Common Core Connection (2.MD)

Grade: Second

Domain: Measurement and Data (MD)

Cluster:

D. Represent and interpret data.

2.MD.D.9. Generate measurement data by measuring lengths of several objects to the nearest whole unit, or by making repeated measurements of the same object. Show the measurements by making a line plot, where the horizontal scale is marked off in whole-number units.

Uncovering Student Understanding About the Key Concepts

Do they

- correspond the value of each X to the number in the scale to determine the numbers in the data set?

OR

- interpret the data set to answer questions?

OR

Do they

- focus only on the data in the scale of the line plot?

- have difficulty interpreting the questions?

Variation 5.3V is the same Probe using a context of number of pets instead of daily temperature.

Exploring Excerpts From Educational Resources and Related Research

Common areas of difficulty for students:

"Analyzing data that are numerical (number of pockets) versus categorical (color of socks) is an added challenge for students as they struggle to make sense of graphs (Russell, 2006). If, for example, the graph has seven stickers above the five, students may think five people have seven stickers or seven people have 5 pockets." (Van de Walle et al., 2013, p. 440)

"In general, comprehension of information in written or symbolic form involves three kinds of behaviors (Jolliffe, 1991; Wood, 1968) that seem to be related to graph comprehension, namely, translation, interpretation, and extrapolation/interpolation." (1) *Translation* requires a change in the form of a communication, (2) *interpretation* requires rearranging material and sorting the important from the less important factors, and (3) *extrapolation* and *interpolation* are considered to be extensions of interpretation, such as noting trends perceived in data. (Friel, Curcio, & Bright, 2001, p. 126)

Surveying the Prompts and Selected Responses in the Probe

If a student chooses	It is likely that the student
1. True 2. True 3. False	• is able to successfully read and interpret the line plot.
1. False	• notices that in the line plot, 73 and 75 both have only one X. (See Sample Student Response 1.)
2. False	• focuses on 73 degrees and sees only one X (see Sample Student Response 2); or • focuses only on temperatures higher than 73 but not including 73 and counts only 4 Xs; or • misinterprets the order of Xs to correspond with the order of the days, thinking the fifth X is the recording from the fifth day, and therefore the temperature was 71 degrees.
3. True	• focuses on the number 74 being 2 greater than the number 72 rather than the number of 72s and 74s in the data set. (See Sample Student Response 3.)

*T*eaching Implications and Considerations

Ideas for eliciting more information from students about their understanding and difficulties:

- To learn more about what the student understands about how to interpret a graph, ask,
  - ○ What do each of the Xs represent in the graph? What do these numbers at the bottom mean?

- For students with correct and incorrect answers, ask questions to learn more about their interpretation of the task as well as their approach:
  - ○ What is this problem about?
  - ○ Can you explain to me what you did to decide on an answer choice?

Ideas for planning instruction in response to what you learned from the results of administering the Probe:

- Students should be active participants in the complete data collection cycle of determining a question, collecting data about the question, analyzing the collected data, and interpreting the results. A focus on using graphs to organize the data for analysis and interpretation is critical.
- After plenty of experiences in generating the data, work with producing line plots can continue with data sets that are provided to the students. At this point focus can shift to discussions about the data by interpreting the line plots.
- Provide data sets and line plots, and ask students to determine which line plot represents which of the data sets, and how they determined the matches.

Sample Student Responses to Reading Line Plots

Responses That Suggest Difficulty

Sample Student Response 1: False. 1 X above the 73 and the 75 not just the 75.

Sample Student Response 2: False: the X above the 73 means 1 time.

Sample Student Response 3: True: 74 is 2 more hotter than 72.

Reading Line Plots: Number of Pets

5.3V

The line plot shows how many pets the students in Mrs. French's class have.

```
                    X
                    X       X
                    X       X               X
            X       X       X               X
            X       X       X       X       X       X
            _____

            0       1       2       3       4       5
                          Number of Pets
```

Decide if each of the following statements about the data are true or false.

	True False
1. 1 student has 5 pets.	True False
Explain why:	

	True False
2. 5 students have 4 or more pets.	True False
Explain why:	

	True False
3. The number of students with 4 pets is 2 greater than the number of students with 3 pets.	True False
Explain why:	

6

Geometry Probes

The content of the Probes in this chapter aligns with the geometry standards for kindergarten and first grade. All of these Probes will also be relevant for students in second grade who have not yet met these kindergarten and first grade standards.

We developed these Probes to address the critical areas of focus in measurement for grades K and 1, described in the standards (CCSSO, 2010) as follows.

Grade K: Describing shapes and space

Students describe their physical world using geometric ideas (e.g., shape, orientation, spatial relations) and vocabulary. They

- identify, name, and describe basic two-dimensional shapes, such as squares, triangles, circles, rectangles, and hexagons, and
- three-dimensional shapes, such as cubes, cones, cylinders, and spheres.
- use basic shapes and spatial reasoning to model objects in their environment and to construct more complex shapes.

Grade 1: Reasoning about attributes of, and composing and decomposing geometric shapes

Students

- compose and decompose plane or solid figures.
- build understanding of part–whole relationships as well as the properties of the original and composite shapes.

The content of the Probes in this chapter align with the geometry standards for kindergarten and first grade. All of these Probes will also be relevant for students in grade two who have not yet met these kindergarten and first grade standards.

- recognize shapes from different perspectives and orientations, describe their geometric attributes, and determine how they are alike and different.

The standards and their related questions, as well as the Probes associated with them, are shown in the table below.

Common Core Math Content

Common Core Mathematical Content	Related Question	Probe Name
Identify and describe shapes (squares, circles, triangles, rectangles, hexagons, cubes, cones, cylinders, and spheres). Analyze, compare, create, and compose shapes. **K.G.A.2, K.G.B.4**	What do students understand about the attributes of a triangle?	Is It a Triangle? (p. 150)
Identify and describe shapes. Analyze, compare, create, and compose shapes. **K.G.A.3, K.G.B.4**	Can students identify shapes as two dimensional or three dimensional and describe attributes of the shapes?	Is It Two Dimensional or Three Dimensional? (p. 159)
Distinguish between defining attributes (e.g., triangles are closed and three-sided) versus non-defining attributes (e.g., color, orientation, overall size); build and draw shapes to possess defining attributes. **K.G.A.1**	What attributes do students focus on when determining similarities and differences among shapes in a collection of shapes?	Odd Shape Out (p. 165)
Partition circles and rectangles into two and four equal shares, describe the shares using the words *halves*, *fourths*, and *quarters*, and use the phrases *half of*, *fourth of*, and *quarter of*. **1.G.A.3**	When given a whole, can students identify when one half of the whole is shaded?	Coloring One Half (p. 170)

This chapter also includes one variation Probe that addresses geometry content and provides an extension to the original Probe Coloring One Half. You'll find this variation Probe at the end of the chapter after the Teacher Notes for the original Probe.

Is It a Triangle? Card Sort Probe

(Reproducible student cards follow Teacher Notes on p. 155)

Triangle	NOT a Triangle		

Advance Preparation: Create cards by photocopying on card stock and cutting. Separate the two blank cards and the two label cards from the deck, and shuffle the rest of the cards.

Instructions:

1. Invite the student(s) to sort the cards into two piles: **Triangle** and **NOT a Triangle**. Use the label cards to identify the piles.

2. As students finish the sort, give them the blank cards, and ask them to create their own **Triangle** and **NOT a Triangle** cards.

3. Ask students to choose three cards from the **Triangle** pile (or choose three cards for them). Ask them to explain or show how they knew these cards should go in the **Triangle** pile.

4. Ask students to choose three cards from the **NOT a Triangle** pile (or choose three cards for them). Ask them to explain or show how they knew these cards should go in the **NOT a Triangle** pile. Use the recording sheet as appropriate.

Teacher Notes:
Is It a Triangle?

Questions to Consider About the Key Mathematical Concepts

What do students understand about the attributes of a triangle? To what extent do they

- understand that triangles have three straight sides and three vertices ("corners")?
- focus on the attributes of the shape rather than simply describing how a shape is similar to a familiar object?

Common Core Connection (K.G)

Grade: Kindergarten

Domain: Geometry

Clusters:

A. Identify and describe shapes (squares, circles, triangles, rectangles, hexagons, cubes, cones, cylinders, and spheres).

K.G.A.2. Correctly name shapes regardless of their orientations or overall size.

B. Analyze, compare, create, and compose shapes.

K.G.B.4. Analyze and compare two- and three-dimensional shapes, in different sizes and orientations, using informal language to describe their similarities, differences, parts (e.g., number of sides and vertices or "corners") and other attributes (e.g., having sides of equal length).

Uncovering Student Understanding About the Key Concepts

Using the Is It a Triangle? Probe can provide the following information about how the students are thinking about iteration.

Do they

- focus on numbers of sides and corners to determine whether a shape is a triangle?

- apply the same definition of a triangle even if the position or orientation is "upside down" or unfamiliar?

Do they

OR
- focus on how similar the shape looks to a familiar shape?

OR
- correctly identify only those triangles in more "typical" positions as triangles?

Do they

- use mathematical language pertaining to the attribute to explain why a shape is an example or a nonexample of a triangle?

OR

Do they

- use words like *slanty, pointy, skinny,* et cetera?

Exploring Excerpts From Educational Resources and Related Research

Common areas of difficulty for students:

Children generally enter school with a great deal of knowledge about shapes. They can identify circles quite accurately and squares fairly well as early as age four. They are less accurate at recognizing triangles (about 60% correct) and rectangles (about 50% correct). Given conventional instruction, which tends to elicit and verify this prior knowledge, children generally fail to make much improvement in their knowledge of shapes from preschool through the elementary grades. (NRC, 2001, p. 284)

"Children begin forming concepts of shape long before they begin formal schooling. The primary grades are an ideal time to help them refine and extend their understandings. Students first learn to recognize a shape by its appearance as a whole or through qualities such as 'pointiness.' They may believe that a given figure is a rectangle because 'it looks like a door.'" (NCTM, 2000, p. 97)

Children at different levels think about shapes in different ways, and they construe such words as *square* with different meanings. To the prerecognition thinker, *square* may mean only a prototypical, horizontal square. To the visual thinker, *squares* might mean a variety of shapes that "look like a perfect box" no matter which way they are rotated. To a descriptive thinker, a square should be a closed figure with four equal sides and four right angles. But even to this child, the square has no relationship to the class of rectangles, as it does for thinkers at higher levels. These levels can help us understand how children think about shapes. (Clements & Sarama, 2007, p. 482)

Surveying the Prompts and Selected Responses in the Probe

There are 10 cards, 5 **Triangle** cards and 5 **NOT a Triangle** cards. The included examples and nonexamples are designed to elicit understandings and common difficulties as described below:

If a student	It is likely that the student
excludes a **Triangle** card:	• focuses on orientation: Shape is positioned "upside down" or "sideways" or is "slanted." (See Sample Student Response 1.)

If a student	It is likely that the student
	• focuses on size: The shape is too "pointy" or "skinny."
includes a **NOT a Triangle** card:	• doesn't realize that a triangle must have straight lines. • doesn't understand that a triangle must be closed (hence the vertices). • extends or straightens the existing lines to correct the shape, since it is "almost" a triangle. (See Sample Student Response 2.) • draws additional lines that result in multiple triangles or seeing two triangles created by the crossed lines. (See Sample Student Response 3.)

Teaching Implications and Considerations

Ideas for eliciting more information from students about their understanding and difficulties:

- Consider the different attributes when choosing cards for explanations. If time allows, ask about more than just three cards from each pile.
- Ask students to give a definition of a triangle; listen for how the student talks about the sides and corners.
- If students describe nonstandard orientations of the figure using words such as *sideways, upside down,* and so on, follow up by asking, "So does that make it a Triangle or NOT a Triangle?"

Ideas for planning instruction in response to what you learned from the results of administering the Probe:

- Very young children can learn rich concepts about shape if provided with varied examples and nonexamples, discussions about shapes and their characteristics, and interesting tasks. Research indicates that curricula should ensure that children experience many different examples of a type of shape. For example, showing a rich variety of triangles and distractors would be likely to generate discussion. Showing nonexamples to compare with similar examples can help to focus attention on the critical attributes (Clements & Sarama, 2004, p. 285).
- Help students build a definition of a triangle by exploring each of the attributes.

Sample Student Responses to Is It a Triangle?

Responses That Suggest Difficulty

Sample Student Response 1

Student: (places in NOT a Triangle pile)

Teacher: Why did you place the card in that pile?

Student: It's upside down.

Teacher: Is it still a triangle even though it is upside down?

Student: No.

Sample Student Response 2

Student: (places in Triangle pile)

Teacher: Why did you place the card in that pile?

Student: It looks like a triangle.

Teacher: Why does it look like a triangle?

Student: (traces over the lines but draws one straight line across the bottom two sides) There's the triangle.

Sample Student Response 3

Student: (places in Triangle pile)

Teacher: Why did you place the card in that pile?

Student: (draws lines on shape) I count five triangles.

Teacher: Is the whole shape a triangle?

Student: Yes.

Responses That Suggest Understanding

Student: (places in NOT A Triangle pile)

Teacher: Why did you place the card in that pile?

Student: (points to curved portion) This isn't straight.

Teacher: Why does that make it NOT a Triangle?

Student: It needs three straight-across sides that touch at three corners.

Is It a Triangle? Reproducible Cards

6.1a

Triangle	NOT a Triangle

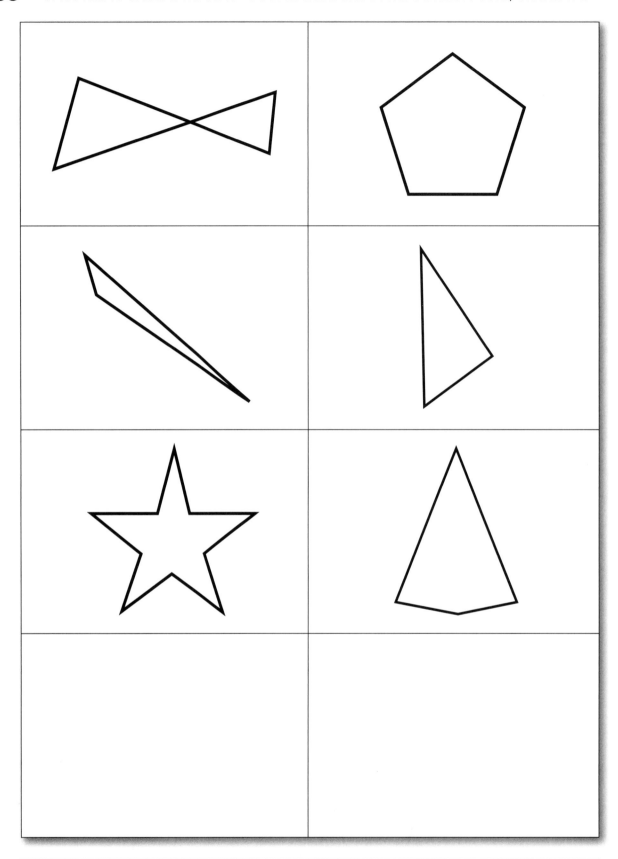

Recording Sheet
Triangles

Card 1 (Tape card to sheet or draw it.)	Show Why
Card 2 (Tape card to sheet or draw it.)	Show Why
Card 3 (Tape card to sheet or draw it.)	Show Why

Recording Sheet
NOT a Triangles

6.1c

Card 1 (Tape card to sheet or draw it.)	Show Why
Card 2 (Tape card to sheet or draw it.)	Show Why
Card 3 (Tape card to sheet or draw it.)	Show Why

Is It Two Dimensional or Three Dimensional?

(Student Interview; reproducible student cards follow Teacher Notes on p. 164)

Two-Dimensional Shapes	Three-Dimensional Shapes

Advance Preparation: Create cards by photocopying on card stock and cutting. Separate the label cards (Two-Dimensional Shapes & Three-Dimensional Shapes) from the deck and shuffle the rest of the cards.

Instructions:

Invite the student to sort the cards into two piles: **Two-Dimensional Shapes** and **Three-Dimensional Shapes.** Use the label cards to identify the piles.

When the student has finished sorting all the cards, ask the following questions, and record the student's responses.

How did you decide which shapes are two dimensional and which shapes are three dimensional?

Choose two cards, one from each group, that you think are related in some way. Why did you choose this pair of cards? (If students choose two that are colored and two that are white, encourage them to try to find cards that are related in a way other than color.)

Choose ANY two cards that you think are very different from one another. Why did you choose this pair of cards?

Teacher Notes: Is It Two Dimensional or Three Dimensional?

Questions to Consider About the Key Mathematical Concepts

Can students identify shapes as two dimensional or three dimensional and describe attributes of the shapes? To what extent do they

- apply geometric and spatial knowledge to distinguish two-dimensional shapes from three-dimensional shapes?
- notice common and unique attributes of these shapes?
- identify the two-dimensional shapes that form the surfaces of three-dimensional shapes?

Common Core Connection (K.G)

Grade: Kindergarten

Domain: Geometry

Clusters:

A. **Identify and describe shapes (squares, circles, triangles, rectangles, hexagons, cubes, cones, cylinders, and spheres).**

  K.G.A.3. Identify shapes as two dimensional (lying in a plane, "flat") or three dimensional ("solid").

B. **Analyze, compare, create, and compose shapes.**

  K.G.B.4. Analyze and compare two- and three-dimensional shapes, in different sizes and orientations, using informal language to describe their similarities, differences, parts (e.g., number of sides and vertices or "corners") and other attributes (e.g., having sides of equal length).

Uncovering Student Understanding About the Key Concepts

Using the Is It Two Dimensional or Three Dimensional? Probe can provide information about how the student is thinking about what distinguishes these two categories of geometric shapes.

Do they

- visualize a three-dimensional shape when it is represented in a two-dimensional picture, and distinguish between the shape and its picture?

OR

Do they

- sort the shapes by an attribute other than dimensionality?

Do they

- describe differences and similarities   OR
between two-dimensional and
three-dimensional shapes by
  - using informal language to
  describe attributes?
  - recognizing two-dimensional
  shapes contained within three-
  dimensional shapes?

Do they

- have difficulty
discerning or
describing differences
between shapes?

Exploring Excerpts From Educational Resources and Related Research

Common areas of development or difficulty for students:

"Spatial sense includes the ability to visualize mentally objects and spatial relationships—to turn things around in your mind. We now know that rich experiences with shape and spatial relationships, when provided consistently over time, can and do develop spatial sense. Without geometric experiences, most people do not grow in their spatial sense or spatial reasoning." (Van de Walle, 2007, p. 408)

"Spatial sense is an intuitive feel for one's surroundings and the objects in them. To develop spatial sense, children must have many experiences that focus on geometric relationships: the direction, orientation, and perspectives of objects in space, the relative shape and sizes of figures and objects, and how a change in shape relates to a change in size." (NCTM, 2001, p. 49)

"Naming shapes is important, but even more important is observing the attributes, or characteristics of shapes." (NCTM, 2001, p. 9)

Research has shown that some students' abilities with geometric concepts are stronger than their number skills. For this reason, tapping into these strengths with geometry and spatial sense can inspire interest in mathematics and provide a context for developing number concepts. (Razel & Eylon, 1991)

Surveying the Prompts and Selected Responses in the Probe

This Probe is a card sort that includes a collection of 16 images of two- and three-dimensional shapes. The items are designed to elicit understandings and common difficulties as described below.

If a student	*It is likely that the student*
sorts the cards accurately into piles	• is able to visualize three dimensions even in drawings of three-dimensional shapes and distinguish them from drawings of two-dimensional shapes.

If a student	It is likely that the student
places some cards in the wrong pile	• is not familiar with some less common shapes or depictions, such as the pyramid with the dotted lines or the cylinder. • sorts by another attribute, such as shapes that are filled in or shaded and those that are not, or curved sides versus straight sides. (See Sample Student Response 1.)
selects two shapes with similar attributes	• is able to identify two-dimensional shapes within three-dimensional shapes. (See Sample Student Response 2.)

Teaching Implications and Considerations

Ideas for eliciting more information from students about their understanding and difficulties:

- To learn more about how the student distinguishes two- and three-dimensional shapes, ask questions that encourage the student to generalize:
    o How did you decide which shapes are two dimensional and which shapes are three dimensional?
    o How would you describe how two-dimensional and three-dimensional shapes are different from one another?
- To learn more about the student's approach and thinking, ask questions related to their placement of the cards:
    o Choose two cards, one from each group, that you think are related in some way. Why did you choose this pair of cards? (If students choose two that are colored and two that are white, encourage them to try to find cards that are related in a way other than color.)
    o Choose ANY two cards that you think are very different from one another. Why did you choose this pair of cards?
    o Are there any cards that you are not sure about?

Students may describe the two-dimensional shapes as flat and the three-dimensional shapes as not flat. They may also compare the three-dimensional shapes to other objects they know, such as a box or a ball. Responses of this nature all reflect good thinking about two-dimensional and three-dimensional shapes.

Ideas for planning instruction in response to what you learned from the results of administering the Probe:

- Use physical materials, drawings, and computer models—students may need more experiences with concrete three-dimensional objects to build their visualization skills. Providing foldable cutout nets of three-dimensional shapes is a strategy for building connections between two- and three-dimensional shapes.

- Provide materials that encourage students to explore geometric shapes. Have students sort and compare blocks or use common items such as cereal boxes and coffee cans to explore attributes of shapes (NCTM, 2000, p. 97).
- Provide opportunities for students to "create mental images of geometric shapes using spatial memory and spatial visualization" (NCTM, 2000, p. 96). Ask students to imagine a particular three-dimensional shape and then to picture in their minds what that shape would look like if it were rotated in space.

Sample Student Responses to Is It Two Dimensional or Three Dimensional?

Responses That Suggest Difficulty

Sample Student Response 1

Student sorts the oval and the circle into the three-dimensional pile.

Teacher: (pointing to these two cards) How did you decide which pile to put these cards in?

Student: I put these here because they are curvy.

Teacher: Could you say some more about how they are curvy?

Student: See how this curves (puts fingers along the outside of the circle), and this one (points to the square) is not.

Responses That Suggest Understanding

Sample Student Response 2

When asked to pick two cards, one from each pile, that are related in some way, the student choose the circle from his two-dimensional pile and the cone from his three-dimensional pile.

Teacher: Why have you chosen these two shapes?

Student: Well this one is a circle, and this one is a circle with a point at the top. So they both have circles but this one (pointing to cone) is 3-D.

Two-Dimensional and Three-Dimensional Shape Sorting Cards

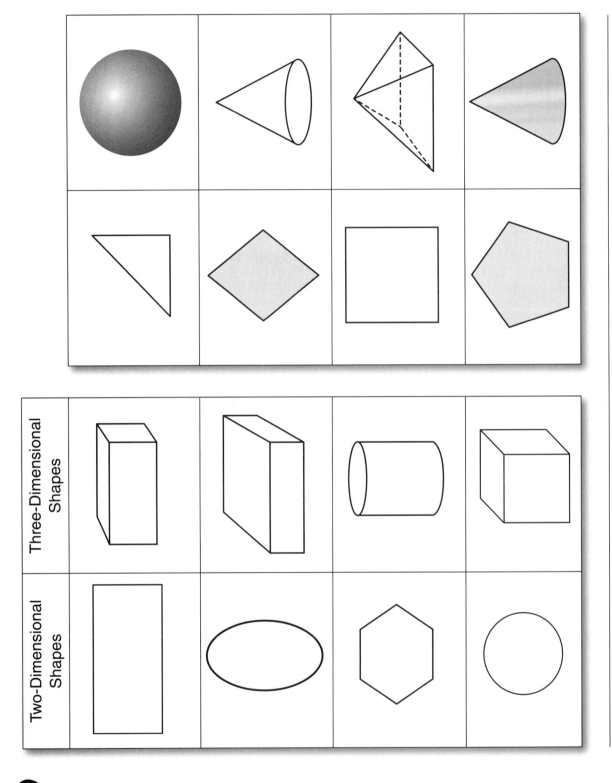

Two-Dimensional Shapes	Three-Dimensional Shapes

6.2a

164

Odd Shape Out

Look at the group of shapes. Put an X over the shape that doesn't belong in the group.

1.	Tell Why
2.	Tell Why
3.	Tell Why

Teacher Notes: Odd Shape Out

Questions to Consider About the Key Mathematical Concepts

What attributes do students focus on when determining similarities and differences among a collection of shapes? To what extent do they

- recognize and characterize two-dimensional shapes by their properties?
- look for multiple similarities and differences, seeing beyond the orientation and size, and thinking instead about the number of sides and vertices ("corners") and relationships among the lengths of the sides?

Common Core Connection (1.G)

Grade: First

Domain: Geometry

Cluster:

A. Reason with shapes and their attributes.

1.G.A.1. Distinguish between defining attributes (e.g., triangles are closed and three sided) versus nondefining attributes (e.g., color, orientation, overall size); build and draw shapes to possess defining attributes.

Uncovering Student Understanding About the Key Concepts

Using the Odd Shape Out Probe can provide the following information about how the students compare attributes of two-dimensional shapes.

Do they		*Do they*
• look for similarities and differences based on the number of sides of the shapes?	OR	• consider other aspects, such as ○ sizes of the shapes? ○ familiarity with particular shapes? ○ orientation of the shapes?
• use mathematical language pertaining to attributes of the shape?	OR	• use words like *slanty, pointy, skinny*, et cetera?

Exploring Excerpts From Educational Resources and Related Research

Common areas of difficulty for students:

"As young learners, we may have identified shapes by memorizing specific attributes, which we may not have fully understood. When memorization occurs without an attachment to well-developed concepts, learners use or hear erroneous terminology that can lead to misconceptions. Likewise, when young learners are offered only regular or common examples of shapes, they connect one label to one shape, which limits applicability and understanding." (Oberdorf & Taylor-Cox, 1999, p. 341)

Children begin forming concepts of shape long before they begin formal schooling. The primary grades are an ideal time to help them refine and extend their understandings. Students first learn to recognize a shape by its appearance as a whole or through qualities such as "pointiness." They may believe that a given figure is a rectangle because "it looks like a door." (NCTM, 2000, p. 39)

"By the time the youngest children begin formal schooling, they have already formed many concepts of shape, although their understanding is largely at the level of recognizing shapes by their general appearance and they frequently describe shapes in terms of familiar objects such as a box or ball." (NCTM, 2001, p. 2)

Students at Level 1 of van Hiele levels of geometric thinking "recognize shapes only as wholes and cannot form mental images of them." Students do not think about the attributes of shapes and instead include "imprecise visual qualities and irrelevant attributes, such as orientation, in describing the shapes." (NCTM, 2003, p. 152)

Surveying the Prompts and Selected Responses in the Probe

The Probe consists of four items, each with four shapes. The collection of examples and the one nonexample in each item is designed to elicit understandings and common difficulties as described below:

If a student chooses	It is likely that the student is
1. ⬡ 2. ⬠ 3. ▽ (correct answers)	• characterizing the two-dimensional shapes by the number of sides and/or corners, and eliminating the shapes with a different number of sides than the others in the group.

If a student chooses	*It is likely that the student is*
Item 1:	• noticing that the shape is smaller in size, and/or • noticing that the shape is the only one "pointing" down. (See Sample Student Response 1.)
Item 2:	• focusing on the orientation (only one "slanted"). (See Sample Student Response 2.)
Item 2:	• noticing that the shape is smaller in size. (See Sample Student Response 2.)
Item 3:	• noticing that the shape is smaller in size. (See Sample Student Response 2.)
Item 3:	• focusing on orientation (the only one "pointing up").

Note: Students who focus on the number of sides may or may not be able to correctly name the shapes.

Teaching Implications and Considerations

Ideas for eliciting more information from students about their understanding and difficulties:

- If the student does not focus on the number of sides or corners, ask, Is there another way to choose a different shape for a different reason?
- If the student does focus on the number of sides or corners, ask, Can you create another shape that would belong with these?

Ideas for planning instruction in response to what you learned from the results of administering the Probe:

- Provide frequent hands-on experiences with materials that help students focus on the attributes of shapes other than size, color, and orientation.
- Give examples of shapes using various orientations.
- Incorporate a range of sorting activities, sometimes giving the categories to students and other times allowing the students to create the categories.

- Educators should keep these several key elements in mind as they introduce and teach geometry concepts to young children: (1) Emphasize the properties and characteristics of a concept; (2) provide many examples and nonexamples, even if the child is not ready to specifically name the nonexamples; (3) pay close attention to language use; and (4) challenge understanding and broaden generalizations (Oberdorf & Taylor-Cox, 1999, pp. 342–343).

Sample Student Responses to Odd Shape Out

Responses That Suggest Difficulty

Sample Student Response 1

Student: This one. It is pointing down this way.

Teacher: Is there a different shape you might pick for a different reason?
Student: No, that's the only one.

Sample Student Response 2

Student: (puts an X over this shape)

Teacher: Why is this shape different?
Student: See how it's tilted. These ones aren't tilted.
Teacher: Is there a different shape you might pick for a different reason?
Student: Could do the small one probably.

Responses That Suggest Understanding

Sample Student Response 3

Student: Count the number of sides. X out the one that's different.
Teacher: Why did you decide to always count the sides?
Student: You have to count the sides to know shapes like triangles, squares, octagons.

Coloring One Half

Students in Mr. Smith's class were asked to color in one half of the picture of the box.

Look at each picture in the table below, and determine whether the student colored in one half of the picture.

Circle Yes or No		Explain Your Thinking
1. 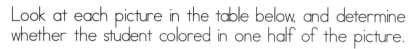	Yes No	
2.	Yes No	
3.	Yes No	
4.	Yes No	
5.	Yes No	

Teacher Notes: Coloring One Half

Questions to Consider About the Key Mathematical Concepts

When given a whole, can students identify when one half of the whole is shaded? To what extent do they

- identify fractional parts in area models when the parts are of equal size but not necessarily the same shape or orientation?
- identify fractional parts in area models when the parts are not contiguous (shaded parts are not adjacent)?

Common Core Connection (1.G)

Grade: First

Domain: Geometry

Cluster:

A. Reason with shapes and their attributes.

1.G.A.3. Partition circles and rectangles into two and four equal shares, describe the shares using the words *halves*, *fourths*, and *quarters*, and use the phrases *half of*, *fourth of*, and *quarter of*. Describe the whole as two of, or four of the shares. Understand for these examples that decomposing into more equal shares creates smaller shares.

Uncovering Student Understanding About the Key Concepts

Using the Coloring One Half Probe can provide the following information about how students are thinking about partitioning.

Do they

- correctly determine which of the colored-in pictures represent one half of the rectangle by visualizing when the picture shows two equal-sized parts with one of the two parts shaded?

OR

Do they

- choose only pictures that show one of the two parts shaded as a rectangle?

- extend this idea by noticing that when there are 4 congruent parts with two parts shaded, the two shaded parts and two unshaded parts can be combined to show that one half of the rectangle is shaded?

OR

- not consider pictures divided into more than two parts?

Variation 6.4V is a similar Probe in structure, but it uses one third instead of one half.

Exploring Excerpts From Educational Resources and Related Research

Common areas of difficulty for students:

Using phrases such as "one out of two" or "one over three" when referring to part–whole relationships can contribute to student confusion. These phrases involve not only different language from that of partitioning but different images as well. (Siebert & Gaskin, 2006, p. 397)

Learning Pitfall: Applying whole number knowledge inappropriately to fractions. For example, students may look for one shaded out of two parts without understanding the need for congruent parts. (Bay Area Mathematics Task Force, 1999, p. 64)

"Although many students start with an intuitive notion of creating equal shares, they typically have only a rudimentary knowledge of how to quantify the results of such partitioning. As children learn to represent the results of equal-sharing problems using part–whole models, they learn to talk about the size of the pieces within those models." (Empson, 1999, p. 330)

Young students tend to focus on shape, when the focus should be equal-*sized* parts. (Van de Walle, Karp, & Bay-Williams, 2013, p. 296)

Surveying the Prompts and Selected Responses in the Probe

The Probe consists of five yes-or-no items. The examples and nonexamples are designed to elicit understandings and common difficulties as described below:

If a student chooses	*It is likely that the student*
Yes on items 1, 2, 4, and 5 (correct answers)	• is using knowledge of part–whole relationships using a rectangular area model. The student understands the represented parts must be of equal size but not necessarily the same shape or orientation, or contiguous.
Yes on Item 3	• believes that one half is one part shaded out of two parts and is not yet paying attention to the size of the parts. (See Sample Student Response 1.)
No on Item 2	• is not familiar with noncontiguous parts. (See Sample Student Response 2.)
No on Item 4	• is not familiar with either the orientation of the parts or with nonrectangular parts. (See Sample Student Response 3.)

Teaching Implications and Considerations

Ideas for eliciting more information from students about their understanding and difficulties:

- For those who choose Yes for all of the items that show one half but do not explain their thinking in terms of part–whole or equal-share language, request: Explain how you decided that these pictures show one half colored in.
- For those who choose Yes for Item 3, focus their attention on the size of the parts, and allow them to reconsider their choice.
- For those who choose No for Item 2, follow up through instructional opportunities that allow the manipulation of the parts.

Ideas for planning instruction in response to what you learned from the results of administering the Probe:

- "The first goal in the development of fractions should be to help students construct the idea of fractional parts of the whole—the parts that result when the whole or unit has been portioned into equal-sized portions or fair shares." Since students make connections between the idea of fair shares and fractional parts, sharing tasks are good places to begin the development of fractions (Van de Walle et al., 2013, p. 295).
- Sharing activities can be used to illustrate concepts such as halves, thirds, and fourths, as well as more general concepts relevant to fractions, such as that increasing the number of people among whom an object is divided results in a smaller fraction of the object for each person. Similarly, early understanding of proportions can help kindergartners compare, for example, how one third of the areas of a square, rectangle, and circle differ (Siegler et al., 2010, pp. 8–9).
- Pattern blocks and fraction circles pieces are common area model manipulatives that can be used in equal-sharing problem contexts.
- Grid models can help students begin to develop the notion of different shape but same size partitioning of thirds and fourths.

Sample Student Responses to Coloring One Half

Responses That Suggest Difficulty

Sample Student Response 1

  Student circles Yes and says, There are 2 parts with this part colored in.

(Continued)

(Continued)

Sample Student Response 2

 Student circles No and says: There are 2 here and 2 here.

Sample Student Response 3

 Student circles No, draws a horizontal line across the middle of the square, and says, You has to be a straight line.

Responses That Suggest Understanding

Sample Student Response 3

 Student circles Yes, outlines a horizontal line across the middle of the square, and says, Both are the same line.

Coloring One Third

Students in Mr. Smith's class were asked to color in one third of the picture of the box.

Look at each picture in the table below, and determine whether the student colored in one third of the picture.

Circle Yes or No		Explain Your Thinking
	Yes No	
	Yes No	
	Yes No	
	Yes No	
	Yes No	

7

Additional Considerations

An assessment activity can help learning if it provides information that teachers and their students can use as feedback in assessing themselves and one another and in modifying the teaching and learning activities in which they are engaged. (Black, Harrison, Lee, Marshall, & Wiliam, 2004, p. 10)

Mathematics assessment Probes represent an approach to diagnostic assessment. They can be used for formative assessment purposes if the information about students' understandings and misunderstandings is used in a way that moves students' learning forward. There is a wide range of considerations included in this chapter, including using the Probes to

- establish learning targets.
- allow for individual reflection.
- give student interviews.
- address individual needs.
- promote math talk.
- support the mathematical practices.
- build capacity among teachers within and across grade levels.

Since the first Uncovering Student Thinking resource was in development, we have worked with and learned from the many teachers who have implemented our assessment Probes or have developed their own assessment Probes to use in their classrooms. Observing classes, trying out strategies ourselves with students, and listening to teachers describe their experiences and approaches have helped us capture various images from practice over time. The vignettes that accompany each of the considerations are chosen to highlight features of a particular instructional approach.

ESTABLISHING LEARNING TARGETS

Stating and sharing intended outcomes of learning and assessment is really the foundation for all formative assessment activities. (Wylie et al., 2012, p. 22)

Establishing learning targets and sharing criteria for success in meeting the targets is the foundation of the embedded formative assessment process (CCSSO, 2008; Heritage, 2010; McManus, 2008; Wiliam, 2011; Wylie et al., 2012). The need to develop students' content knowledge, including knowledge of the important mathematics concepts, procedures, and skills outlined in the Common Core Mathematical Standards and Practices, is a priority for mathematics educators. In order for students to meet these established expectations, instruction and assessment must take place with a clear learning target in mind. Standards should inform teachers' thinking about learning targets as an interconnected cluster of learning goals that develop over time. By clarifying the specific ideas and skills described in the standards and articulating them as specific lesson-level learning targets aligned to criteria for success, teachers are in a better position to uncover the gap between students' existing knowledge or skill and the knowledge or skill described in the learning target and criteria for success.

Assessment Probe Use Related to Learning Targets

Each assessment Probe addresses a key mathematical concept related to a Common Core mathematics content standard(s), providing an example of how subsets of mathematics standards can be developed as learning goals. The example in Figure 7.1, from the Completing Number Sentences Probe, highlights three components of the Teacher Notes helpful in determining learning targets: Uncovering Student Understanding, Questions to Consider About the Key Mathematic Concepts, and the connections to the Common Core Standards.

Figure 7.1 Excerpts From Teacher Notes for Completing Number Sentences

Questions to Consider About the Key Mathematical Concepts

Do students apply an understanding of equality and the operation of addition to determine the missing value in an equation? To what extent do they

- think flexibly about equations and the meaning of the equal sign?
- demonstrate an understanding of the operation of addition and foundational number concepts related to addition?

(Continued)

Figure 7.1 (Continued)

Common Core Connection (OA)

Grade: First

Domain: Operations and Algebraic Thinking (OA)

Cluster:

Work with addition and subtraction equations.

1.OA.D.7. Understand the meaning of the equal sign, and determine if equations involving addition and subtraction are true or false. For example, which of the following equations are true and which are false? $6 = 6$, $7 = 8 - 1$, $5 + 2 = 2 + 5$, $4 + 1 = 5 + 2$.

1.OA.D.8. Determine the unknown whole number in an addition or subtraction equation relating three whole numbers. For example, determine the unknown number that makes the equation true in each of the equations $8 + ? = 11$, $5 = \_\_\_ - 3$, $6 + 6 = \_\_\_$.

 Uncovering Student Understanding
About the Key Concepts

Using the Completing Number Sentences Probe can provide information about how students are thinking about equality and the meaning of the equal sign.

Do they

- correctly interpret aspects of the equation, such as
  - the addends?
  - the equal sign?
  - the box symbol representing the missing value?

- apply an understanding of the equal sign as a symbol of equality that tells them the quantities on each side have the same value?

- apply number concepts such as hierarchical inclusion, compensation, decomposition, and composition to determine the missing value?

Do they

OR
- add quantities without consideration of all of the numbers and symbols contained in the equation?

OR
- interpret the equal sign as a sort of stop sign that means "when you reach the equal sign, it's time to compute"?

OR
- rely only on counting or counting on to determine a sum?

Note: Have concrete materials such as counters or cubes available to students should they request them to assist them in their problem solving. If students seem to have some knowledge of the tasks but are struggling or frustrated with the computation, consider offering these, but do not offer them from the start.

Many teachers we work with are establishing learning targets on a daily basis and are using the Probes as a tool both to support the development of a learning target prior to a lesson and to help students during a lesson reach the learning target.

When using a Probe to support the development of a learning target prior to a lesson, teachers give the Probe to students one to three days prior to the upcoming lesson or unit of instruction. They analyze the evidence gathered from the assessment to gauge students' current understandings and misunderstandings, and use this information to develop a learning target or set of learning targets.

The following image from practice provides an example of using a Probe prior to the start of a lesson or set of lessons.

In preparation for beginning work with partitioning shapes, I wanted to get a sense of what my students already knew related to the idea. Knowing that many of my students were already thinking in terms of two halves as sharing equal amounts of something between two people, I was interested to see how many students would apply similar reasoning when explaining how they determined whether one half of the picture of the box was colored in. I had the students complete the Probe during our math class time that is set aside for "math practice" activities, in which we do a variety of mental math, facts practice, vocabulary builders, and other activities to provide ongoing content lessons from prior lessons or grades.

After reviewing the students' explanations, I decided on the following:

- I would start with halves, but the focus would be on nonrectangular parts.
- Since two students said yes to the nonequal parts, I made a note on a sticky note to remind myself to touch base with those students during the first lesson to see if the lesson's task helped clarify the misconception. I put the sticky note in my teacher manual for that lesson.
- None of the students said yes on the box with the two of four shaded, but this isn't a goal in our curriculum. I want to build from the understanding of fair sharing that was definitely evident in the majority of their responses, and incorporate some activities for some if not all students to push their thinking about the meaning of partitioning shapes into halves.

Incorporating the Probe prior to preparing for a unit, especially one that is new to our curriculum, helped confirm for me that students had the foundational understandings that I had informally observed in various math tasks, and gave me information about a starting point, about which students might need extra support during at least that initial stage, and about what content to consider as an extension to what the activities within the unit allow students to explore.

When using a Probe as a tool within a lesson or set of lessons, teachers first establish an alignment between the Probe content and the established learning target. In addition, they design instructional activities to support predicted understandings and misunderstandings likely to be uncovered by the Probe.

Figure 7.2 Envelopes for Card Sort Probes

I have used card sort Probes previously but wanted to set up a process for more regular use. At the beginning of the school year, I gave each student a small reclosable 6 × 9 manila envelope with two small letter envelopes inside (one labeled *yes* and one labeled *no*). Students wrote their names on the manila envelopes and decorated them (see Figure 7.2).

At times I have the students do the card sort, while I make observations during the sort and then review the cards of students I had questions about at a later time. Other times I use the sort as part of a day's lesson. For example, I had the students sort their Sums of Ten cards at the start of the lesson, while I made observations to consider pairings based on where students were in relation to the learning target.

Student Learning Targets:

I can use my count-on strategy when finding the sum of two or more numbers.

I can explain to a classmate how I used my strategy to find the sum.

I gathered the students in our discussion circle and practiced some subitizing with various dot cards, asking students to share what they noticed. I added to my typical cards three examples of sums with one dot image and one number, and again asked students to share how they got their totals. I repeated this with finding sums given only numbers. After our discussion circle time, I set the students up into pairs and demonstrated how they were going to

1. compare all of the NO cards (NOT sums of ten) and sort them into two piles, agree and disagree (sorting cards each student had in the NO pile into the agree pile, and sorting cards that only one student had in the NO pile into the disagree pile).
2. review the agree cards to decide if you want to keep them in the NO pile.
3. review the disagree cards to decide whether you want to keep the card in the NO pile or move it to the YES pile.
4. repeat the process of determining agreement of the cards with those in the YES pile.

As students finished, I gave them two blank cards each to create an example and nonexample for their partners to place in the correct pile. As the students were working, I made note of cards that showed up in disagree piles and listened to explanations of strategies to determine whether the earlier discussion circle had influenced approaches. I also made note of several student-generated examples and nonexamples to share in our closing discussion circle.

Using the sort as part of the activity of the lesson works well for my students. They are very motivated to compare their sort with that of another student, which also provides an opportunity for them to critique their partner's reasoning and to communicate about their own strategies.

INDIVIDUAL METACOGNITION AND REFLECTION (THE 4 CS)

The Conceptual Change Model begins with having students become aware of their own thinking. Through a series of developmental steps, it helps them to confront their views and to refine them if necessary, then to immediately use their new understanding. (Stepans, Schmidt, Welsh, Reins, & Saigo, 2005, p. 37)

The conceptual change model as described by Stepans and colleagues (2005) takes into consideration recommendations from research and is rooted in the learning cycle approach. The goal of the conceptual change model is to uncover students' current ideas about a topic before teaching new content related to the topic. Students learn by integrating new knowledge with what they already know and can do. Sometimes this new knowledge is integrated in a way that contributes to or builds on an existing misunderstanding. Through the conceptual change approach, since ideas are elicited prior to instruction, existing preconceptions and/or misconceptions can be confronted explicitly, minimizing situations in which students are trying to integrate new knowledge into a flawed or underdeveloped framework of ideas. This explicit confrontation of preconceptions or misconceptions creates cognitive dissonance in which students begin to question and rethink their preconceptions, and further instruction and reflection can now help students understand the new concept. Our 4Cs model, an adaptation of the conceptual change model, consists of four stages, as shown in Figure 7.3.

At this point, you may be wondering how the 4Cs model connects with the QUEST cycle. The QUEST cycle is written from a teacher point of view and implicitly incorporates the 4Cs model. Since even the most effective teachers cannot do the actual learning for their students, the 4Cs model provides the critical student perspective.

Assessment Probe Use Related to the 4Cs Model

Teachers using the 4Cs model in conjunction with assessment Probes typically use the following process:

1. *Commit.* Choose a Probe to elicit ideas related to a learning target. Give the Probe to all students, capturing student responses either by asking students to write explanations, scripting their explanations, or a combination of both.

2. *Confront.* Provide instruction based on results, integrating a variety of anonymous student responses, both correct and incorrect, into the lesson at appropriate junctures, and lead class discussion about the responses.

Figure 7.3   The 4 Cs Model

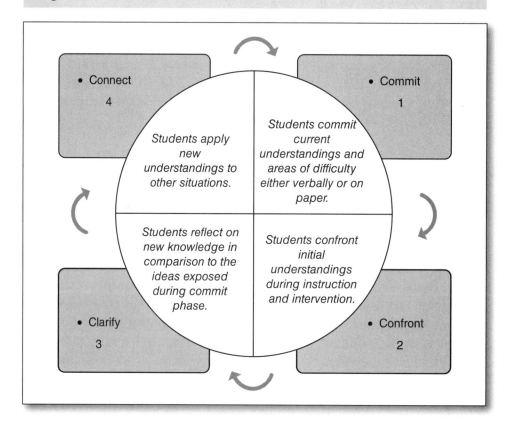

3. *Clarify.* Return students' initial responses to the Probe to them (or read them to students), and ask students to clarify or revise anything in the response based on what they just learned in the lesson.

4. *Connect.* Pose additional questions similar to those in the Probe to assess whether students have met the learning target.

The following image from practice highlights the use of the 4Cs model.

I gave the variation of the Apples and Oranges Probe to my students prior to the unit in which they work a lot with larger sums such as 8, 10, 12, and 15. We had worked on similar situations with smaller numbers, including 4, 5, and 6, so I was curious to see how my students would approach a bigger number and whether they would incorporate some of the strategies we used in the other related tasks. I planned to give the Probe again once we finished the related sections of the unit.

While other stations were working on tasks related to our current content, two pairs of students were asked to work on the Probe. By having two groups in close proximity, I could go between the groups, helping students record their thinking, and annotating when needed. On each group's table I left a bucket of linking cubes, giving students the option to use them if they wanted.

I broke the Probe into two parts by first asking students to complete the problem without knowing that they would then be reviewing three other students' responses. While watching the students generate their lists and helping them record as needed, I was able to observe the number of sentences students were able to generate as well as the approach to generating more than one number sentence. As students or groups of students indicated they were finished, I gave them the second part of the Probe, read aloud the directions, and asked the students to circle their choices and use words to tell why. Again I observed and helped students record explanations. When the students were finished, I had a station task ready for them to go to in another area of the room.

In preparation for the start of the unit, I created a pictograph by enlarging the student faces and showing the number of students who chose each of the responses (Figure 7.4).

In addition to sorting the work by choice, I also categorized the types of strategies students used to find more than one number sentence and added a tally of this information to the poster.

Periodically throughout the series of lessons in the unit, I would point to the chart and ask whether as a class we could rule out any of the answers. When confident that all students could justify eliminating a response, I put an X on each of the faces. I found that many of the students could no longer remember their choices on the Probe, but I held off showing them their original responses until we had crossed out all but one of the choices on the poster. In conjunction with talking about the choices, we also kept track of various strategies for recording all of the combinations and added examples of the strategies to the poster.

When I did give the students back their original responses, I asked them to rework the problem on a new handout. As students worked on their new responses, I moved about to help them read earlier responses and record new ideas.

Finally, toward the end of the unit, I gave the students the Play Ball (Rose Tobey & Minton, 2011, p. 122) Probe variation to look for students' ability to apply their understandings to a new context and larger number.

Figure 7.4 Pictograph Showing Student Responses to Apples and Oranges Probe

GIVING STUDENT INTERVIEWS

> *Whenever we try to get at a student's thinking, we should try to focus not only on what the student is thinking but also on what the student understands about his or her own knowledge. The questions we ask when interviewing a student will help the student become more aware of her own cognitive processes. (Ashlock, 2006, p. 27)*

Conducting individual or small group interviews provides information beyond what written student work can provide. Interviewing students offers insight into their level of understanding and their ability to put mathematical ideas into words and/or representations. The interview process also allows teachers to gather information about the range of learning needs within a group of students. Teachers who regularly incorporate student interviews either selectively interview a subset of students or interview all of their students depending upon how they wish to use the results.

Assessment Probe Use Related to Student Interviews

"Good interviewing requires careful preparation in advance, keeping in mind purposes, method of selection, environment, questions and follow-up Probes, and uses" (Stepans, Schmidt, Welsh, Reins, & Saigo, 2005, p. 277). The student interview is the primary structure for many of the assessment Probes developed for kindergarten and first grade, because students' ability to write their ideas by themselves is limited at this age. Student interviews continue to be important at second grade as well, but because students at this age are more able to express their thinking in written words and symbols, the teacher has additional choices about how to administer the Probes. Teachers have found that any Probe can be administered as an interview and see benefits to this mode of administration at any age.

Many teachers manage individual interviews by conducting them while their students not being interviewed are engaged in other activities. The Apples and Oranges vignette showcases how one teacher utilizes a station approach to enable her to "interview" multiple students individually as they are engaged in the tasks of the Probe. At other times, teachers interview students using a more typical format by pulling one student at a time from a station.

In addition to or in place of individual interviews, teachers also use structured small group interviews during station time. This method allows for individual Level 1 selected responses but, depending on writing capabilities, may rely on a small group discussion for the Level 2 explanations. When managed well, these conversations provide valuable information about both students' thinking and their ability to build on the ideas of other students to advance their thinking. One challenge of the small group interview approach is the temptation to jump from information gathering into instruction. Stay focused on and be explicit with students that the goal of this small group activity is for you to listen to their ideas and ask questions in order to plan for a new learning experience on another day. Being explicit in this way avoids confusion for students who may also participate in small intervention groups or other small group work focused on instruction.

ADDRESSING INDIVIDUAL NEEDS

Although many teachers feel they lack the time or tools to pre-assess on a regular basis, the data derived from pre-assessment are essential in driving differentiated instruction. (Small, 2009, p. 5)

In addition to using Probes as preassessment, understanding how the math content contained in the Probe connects to a progression of math learning can support efforts to differentiate instruction to meet students' needs.

The Common Core State Standards in mathematics were built on progressions: narrative documents describing the progression of a topic across a number of grade levels, informed both by research on children's cognitive development and by the logical structure of mathematics. These documents were spliced together and then sliced into grade level standards. From that point on the work focused on refining and revising the grade level standards. The early drafts of the progressions documents no longer correspond to the current state of the standards.

It is important to produce up-to-date versions of the progressions documents. They can explain why standards are sequenced the way they are, point out cognitive difficulties and pedagogical solutions, and give more detail on particularly knotty areas of the mathematics. (Institute for Mathematics and Education, University of Arizona, 2007)

Being aware of and understanding a progression of learning of a topic is important when considering how to address the needs of students. Often individual students can be grouped with others who have a similar misunderstanding or who have a similar missing foundational concept that is posing a barrier to learning the mathematics of the learning target. "Compiling an inventory for a set of papers can provide a sense of the class's progress and thus inform decisions about how to differentiate instruction" (Burns, 2005, p. 29). Decisions about next steps should be informed based on the goal of moving students' understanding toward a defined learning target, but when the gap between existing knowledge and the learning target is too great, students may need to access the content at a "lower" point in the learning progression. This may require developing alternate and additional learning targets allowing students to build the prerequisite understand necessary. Probes provide critical information to inform these decisions and are therefore a useful tool for all teachers of math, including special educators, Title I teachers, and interventionists.

PROMOTING MATH TALK

Because discussions help students to summarize and synthesize the mathematics they are learning, the use of student thinking is a critical element of mathematical discourse. When teachers help students build on their thinking through talk, misconceptions are made clearer to both teacher and student, and at the same time, conceptual and procedural knowledge deepens. (Garcia, 2012, p. 3)

"Talking the talk is an important part of learning" (Black & Harrison, 2004, p. 4). When students are talking about their mathematical ideas, whether in a whole-class discussion, in small groups, or in pairs, they are using the language and conventions of mathematics.

Children learn vocabulary primarily indirectly through their conversations with others and from the books and programs they are exposed to. However, because many words used in mathematics may not come up in everyday contexts—and if they do, they may mean something totally different—math vocabulary needs to be explicitly taught (Minton, 2007). Students' use of math terms is directly related to their experiences. Lack of exposure to math situations and opportunities to develop a correct mathematical vocabulary can deprive students of the language of math. The language of math is specific and uses not only words to denote meaning but also symbolic notation. Symbols enable mathematical ideas to be expressed in precise ways that reflect quantitative relationships. Misunderstandings about the meaning of a math symbol or notation or how to use it can impact understanding. Just as some words can take on different meanings in different contexts, so can some mathematical symbols.

Assessment Probe Use Related to Promoting Math Talk

In Chapter 1, we used an image from practice to illustrate how assessment Probes can create a link between assessment, instruction, and learning. We remind you of that image here:

In a primary classroom, students are having a "math talk" to decide which figures are triangles. After using a Card Sort strategy to individually group picture cards as "triangles" and "not triangles," the teacher encourages the students to develop a list of characteristics that could be used to decide whether a figure is a triangle. As students share their ideas and come to an agreement, the teacher records the characteristic and draws an example and non example to further illustrate the idea. She then gives students an opportunity to regroup their cards, using the defining characteristics developed as a class. As the students discuss the results of their sorting process, she listens for and encourages students to use the listed characteristics to justify their choices. Throughout the discussion, the class works together to revise the triangle characteristics already listed and to add additional characteristics that were not included in the initial discussion. (Keeley & Rose Tobey, 2011, p. 1)

The image illustrates how a teacher engages students in discussion, using the examples and nonexamples to tease out characteristics of triangles. The book from which this excerpt is taken, *Mathematics Formative Assessment: 75 Practical Strategies for Linking Assessment, Instruction and Learning*, provides descriptions of specific strategies that can be combined with assessment Probes in order to promote learning through mathematical discourse (Keeley & Rose Tobey, 2011). Many of these strategies have been used or modified for use by grade K–2 teachers. Two such strategies, Agreement Circles and the more commonly used Think-Pair-Share, provide a whole group strategy example and a pair/small group example of promoting learning through discourse.

Agreement Circles

Agreement Circles provide a kinesthetic way to activate thinking and engage students in discussing and defending their mathematical ideas. Students stand in a large circle as the teacher reads a statement. The students who agree with the statement step to the center of the circle. Those who disagree remain standing on the outside of the circle. Those in the inner circle face their peers still standing around the outside circle and then divide themselves into small groups of students who agree and disagree. The small groups then engage in discussion to defend their thinking. This is repeated with several rounds of statements relating to the same topic, each time with students starting by standing around the large circle. At the beginning, this strategy works best with Probes that generated substantial disagreement. Over time, once the classroom environment allows for students to take risks and feel safe doing so, the strategy can be successfully used when a smaller range of students choose certain selected responses (Keeley & Rose Tobey, 2011, pp. 54–55).

Think-Square-Share

Think–Pair–Share begins by providing students with an opportunity to activate their own thinking. The pairing strategy allows students to first share their ideas with one other person and modify their ideas or construct new knowledge as they interact with their partner. Next, students are asked to share ideas with a larger group. After having had a chance to discuss their ideas with another student as a pair, many students are more comfortable and willing to respond to the whole group discussion. As a result, the quality of their responses often improves and contributes to an improvement in the quality of the whole group discussion as well. Thoughtful pairing of students helps to ensure that the pair conversation is productive. Consider pairing students with others with whom they will engage productively and whose content-level understanding is similar enough for common ground yet reflects differences that will evoke conversation.

In the Think-Square-Share variation, students discuss in groups of four rather than in pairs. When using a Probe with selected response choices, teachers can prearrange groups so that each includes students who chose different selections. In their "square," they have a chance to discuss their thinking and try to justify their reasoning or modify it based on information they gain from the discussion (Keeley & Rose Tobey, 2011, pp. 189–190).

SUPPORTING THE MATHEMATICAL PRACTICES

Formative assessment begins by identifying a learning goal, based on a grade-level standard from the Common Core State Standards (CCSS). The Common Core State Standards for Mathematics (CCSSM) define what students should understand and be able to do in K–2 mathematics and beyond. Since the grade-level standards in the CCSSM "define what students should understand and be able to do," it is important for teachers to find out what students know and can do both conceptually and procedurally in relation to the expectation for learning. In addition to these content standards, an important feature of the CCSSM is the Standards for Mathematical Practices. These practices describe a variety of processes and proficiencies that teachers at all grade levels should seek to develop in their students. Since the CCSSM do not define the methods and strategies used to determine the readiness and prior knowledge necessary to achieve the standards, the mathematics assessment Probes in this book complement CCSSM's eight Standards for Mathematical Practices and their link to mathematical content (Keeley & Rose Tobey, 2011, p. 30).

How the use of Probes supports each of the Practice Clusters (see Appendix B for more information about these Clusters) is described below, beginning with the Practices related to reasoning and explanation.

Assessment Probe Use Related to the Reasoning and Explaining Practice Cluster

Simply using the mathematics assessment Probes with students will not result in students who are proficient within this cluster of practices. Instead, use of the Probes over time, combined with higher expectations for Level 2 responses elaborating on reasons for selecting a response, will support students as they progress toward proficiency. Use of the follow-up questions accompanying the Probes (see Figure 7.5 for an example) can help students who are having difficulty describing their reasoning or who give only brief explanations such as "I just knew" or "my teacher told me that."

Since young students naturally generalize from examples and nonexamples, many of the assessment Probes are structured or can be structured as card sorts, which capitalize on examples and nonexamples, to help students build important reasoning skills. Primary students are very able to use a variety of ways to justify their answers, including perception, evidence gathered from observation, and short chains of deductive reasoning grounded in previously accepted facts or properties. The extent to which students are able to use these skills when giving explanations can be elicited through use of the Probes.

Many of the assessment Probes make use of the "math-talk" structure, in which students are asked to decide who they agree with and provide a reason for their choice. Probes that are structured in this way provide opportunities for students to critique the reasonableness of another's thinking and justify their findings. Again, using Probes structured in this way only on occasion during the school year will not build students' ability in a meaningful way. Instead, students will need multiple opportunities over the course of the school year and across all of the mathematics domains in order to build these abilities.

Figure 7.5   Are They Equivalent? Follow-Up Questions

*T*eaching Implications and Considerations

Ideas for eliciting more information from students about their understanding and difficulties:

- How did you use estimation and reasoning to decide on your responses?
- In what ways are addition and subtraction alike and different?
- What does it mean for two expressions to be equivalent?
- Can you think of another expression that is equivalent to this one?

After several uses of Probes during learning stations, I began to have students engage in small group discussions about their responses to a particular Probe. I found these short exchanges invaluable for learning about individual students' reasoning and explanation capabilities.

The following exchange is an example of a small group discussion of the Building Numbers Game Probe variation (shown in Figure 3.2Vb).

Me: You each have an answer to the problem and have explained your thinking. I would like you to talk to each other about your answers and explanations. Remember, right now I am listening and questioning to hear your thinking. Later, we will talk more about these types of problems. Mason, can you begin?

Mason: I think he (points to Juan) has the largest number. 82 is the biggest number on any of the cards.

Jayden: I picked Peter. I found all cards with 100s up top and 7 of them is more than 5 or 6 of them.

Mia: I did what Mason did.

Me: Did you do exactly what Mason did? Mason can you say what you did again?

Mason: (points to each of the 9 cards individually) 82 is way bigger than any other number. 16 is the next biggest, but 82 is way more.

Mia: I looked at all the cards just like that. 3 was smallest and 82 was biggest and all these are in the middle of 3 and 82.

Me: What do you think (pointing to number of labels) these mean?

(Continued)

(Continued)

Jayden: It's like those cubes, longs, and flats we have used before. I was thinking of those in my head.

Me: Mason or Mia what can you tell me about those?

Mia: We used them to add numbers last week.

Me: Think about how the cubes, longs, and flats could help us with knowing what numbers Juan, Peter, and Trish have. Without talking more, look at your paper to think about if you want to add anything to your explanation. It is okay to change your answer if you want.

I noticed the following changes as students individually worked.

Mason: Changed his selected response to Peter and added to his explanation, "Now I think I should look at the 100s cards to see which is bigger."

Jayden: Changed her selected response to Trish and added to her explanation, "Mia said about adding with blocks. With 27 + 35 we traded when there was lots of little cubes. So look at 100s and 10s cards and trade."

Mia: Kept her selected response as Juan and added to her explanation, "I looked at all the numbers to find smallest one and biggest one. Biggest one was 82." (Note that previously she had written, "Because he has the biggest number so he should win.")

Since I allow students to change their responses after the discussion, the process also helps me determine the "depth" of the misunderstanding and whether the students were persuaded in any way by listening to the others talk and/or by my follow-up questions.

I often ask students if they agree with a classmate's strategy and/or solution and then follow up by asking several students why they agree or do not agree. This is a regular feature of our daily class discussions during math time and becomes a routine for students.

The "math-talk" Probe structure mirrors this routine in a way that allows all students to respond. When given a math-talk Probe, students first reason about the problem and then compare their thinking and approach to those of several fictitious students. If they agree with one of the fictitious student's responses, they then need to be able to explain *why* they agree.

Periodically using a math-talk Probe "slows down the process," allowing more time for all students to reflect and communicate before they begin to share their thinking. In addition to providing this benefit for students, this Probe structure of "think, compare, choose, and explain" gives me a chance to scan students' choices more quickly to determine who may be struggling for a particular reason and what patterns are emerging across all of the student responses.

I also use this Probe structure to design my own math-talk tasks as miniassessments during or toward the end of a set of lessons. I use actual student responses that I have heard from the students during class discussions to create my own math-talk responses.

"When students derive answers to problems, we not only need to get at their thinking in order to understand how they obtained those answers, we also need to learn how they justify their answers—how they prove they are correct in their own thinking. We can look for three kinds of justification schemes identified by Sowder and Harel and illustrated by Flores:

- *Externally based schemes* in which a textbook or authority figure is cited as justification.
- *Empirically based schemes* in which students use perception or concrete objects to show that their answer is correct.
- *Analysis use schemes* in which students use counting strategies or state mathematical relations to justify their answer.

As a student's thinking develops over time, we expect to see fewer uses of justification schemes that are externally based. We even hope to see use of empirically-based schemes eventually give way to schemes that use analysis, for such thinking is distinctly mathematical." (Ashlock, 2006, p. 28)

In summary, grade K–2 students should be encouraged to make conjectures, be given time to search for evidence to prove or disprove them, and be expected to explain and justify their ideas. Students should be introduced to and be expected to use basic logic words in their explanation, including *not, and, or, all, some, if . . . then,* and *because, and to* incorporate mathematical properties and relationships, rather than authority (e.g., "because my teacher told us"), as the basis for the argument.

Assessment Probe Use Related to the Seeing Structure and Generalizing Practice Cluster

Many of the mathematics targets of the assessment Probes align to the CCSSM content standards directly associated with the Seeing Structure and Generalizing Practice Structure. For example, the Are They Equivalent? Probe (see Figure 7.6) elicits from students whether they understand the commutative property as well as other place value ideas that allow one to check equivalence without actually calculating and comparing the results.

Students who are able to choose the correct responses without calculating are likely to be seeing the structure within each of the problem sets. The Level 2 explanation is key to determining whether, in fact, students are seeing the structure and are able to explain/articulate the reasons for their correct responses.

The Apples and Oranges Probe (see Figure 7.7) elicits whether students are able to systematically find sums of ten in order to determine who they agree with about the number of combinations.

How students approach finding the combinations tells us a lot about their previous experiences and whether they can apply a systematic approach to decompose the number 10. Students who apply a random method of listing numbers may stop before they have reached all possible combinations and have difficulty figuring out what is missing in their list.

Figure 7.6   Are They Equivalent? Probe

Are They Equivalent?

1. Without adding the two numbers, use what you know about adding two-digit numbers to decide which of the number expressions below are equivalent to

23 + 45

	Circle One	Explain Your Answer
A. 25 + 43	Yes No	
B. 24 + 35	Yes No	
C. 32 + 54	Yes No	
D. 45 + 23	Yes No	
E. 20 + 48	Yes No	

Figure 7.7 Apples and Oranges Probe

Apples and Oranges

Sasha is filling a bowl with apples and oranges.

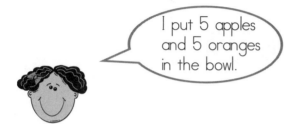

I put 5 apples and 5 oranges in the bowl.

Is there another way to fill this bowl with apples and oranges and have exactly 10 pieces of fruit in it?

YES   NO

Explain your answer. Write number sentences to show your thinking.

Assessment Probe Use Related to the Modeling and Using Tools Practice Cluster

Many of the mathematical targets of the assessment Probes align to the Common Core content standards directly associated with the Modeling and Using Tools Practice Cluster. For example, the Length of Rope Probe (see Figure 7.8) makes use of minicrayons to determine the length of a series of pieces of rope.

Figure 7.8   Length of Rope Probe

Length of Rope

Susie is using minicrayons to measure different-size pieces of rope. The pieces of rope and minicrayons are shown below.

Problems 1–3

Decide if each piece of Susie's rope is 3 minicrayons long.	Circle One
1	Yes No
2	Yes No
3	Yes No

Explain how you decided whether to circle Yes or No:

Problems 4–6

Decide if each piece of Susie's rope is 3 minicrayons long.	Circle One
4	Yes No
5	Yes No
6	Yes No

Explain how you decided whether to circle Yes or No:

How students make use of the minicrayon as a potential tool depends on the foundational conceptual ideas they understand and are able to apply to the Probe context. Once again, it is the Level 2 explanation prompt that requires students to describe their process and allows the teacher to get a better sense of the students' approach and use of tools.

Our measurement unit has a lot of great hands-on activities requiring students to measure with many different-size objects. Students are asked to measure both by using only one object/unit to repeatedly tile the object/unit, and by using multiple objects/units that are all the same size.

When I first saw this Probe, I realized that while I have always given my students a lot of experience with measuring, I wasn't at all sure whether they would be able to transfer those experiences to determine whether the rope was 3 minicrayons long. I was very curious to try the Probe with this class of students and decided to wait to give the Probe until we were midway through the set of measuring activities.

I kept track of the types of issues that would be raised by the Probe and watched for these same difficulties while the students were actually measuring, such as overlapping units, gaps, missing first units, et cetera. I tried to bring out these issues during whole class discussions when possible and even set up some scenarios that would replicate a similar situation. For example, when we were using shoe prints to measure the length of an area rug, I left a gap the size of a shoe print out in the middle of the row before calling the students over to talk about the measure.

When I gave the Probe, I still had a few students who had difficulty with the transition to paper-and-pencil calculating rather than using objects, but many improvised by making something the same length as the minicrayon. Others were able to tell me about how they determined the answer without the actual object. Having this information gave me a sense of how I wanted to structure the remaining measurement activities and who would need more support.

I found having the Probe in mind as a target informed my questioning when I was working with individuals or pairs of students as well as during class discussions of the activities. My teaching was much more focused this year even after having taught the unit for five years previously.

The Solving Number Stories Probe (see Figure 7.9) is an example of a Probe that elicits information about whether students are able to model with mathematics.

Students who can make sense of the sequence of actions within a problem context can determine whether to add or subtract the given numbers. They are able to model the problem correctly and describe how their model and solution relate back to the context as well as the process they used to solve the problem.

In addition to Probes that are directly connected to content standards related to modeling and/or the use of tools, all the assessment Probes have the ability to elicit information regarding this Practice Cluster. For many of the assessment Probes, there is not an expectation that a particular model or tool be used. At the diagnostic stage, more information is gathered about your students if you naturally allow students to request tools to use in determining their response and/or explaining their thinking. For example, when completing the Apples and Oranges Probe, students may or may not ask for concrete materials to model the problem. When students struggle with this task yet do not ask for materials, they may not yet have the skills to be proficient with this particular practice. An important consideration when using assessment Probes is to combine the use of Probes that expect specific modeling processes or given tools with Probes that expect more varied and open-ended approaches. In this way, you can provide opportunities for students to practice identifying and utilizing helpful tools, and you can learn how their abilities in this area are progressing.

Assessment Probe Use Related to the Overarching Habits of Mind of Productive Thinkers Practice Cluster

The assessment Probes support student metacognition by inviting students to identify the extent of their own understanding of a problem and its solution and to examine and make sense of the problem-solving approaches of others. The Probes relate to this overarching cluster of practices both in terms of the content of the Probes and the ways in which they are used in questioning, instruction, and discussion.

Chapter 3 discusses many of these instructional considerations for using Probes as a bridge between assessment, instruction, and learning.

Many of the Probes require precision in the Level 2 explanation that supports a Level 1 selected response. For example, in the Are They Equivalent? Probe variation (see Figure 7.10), students determine whether adding two numbers would give a sum equal to that of 427 + 569. Students who are able to correctly determine yes or no by articulating ideas related to math properties are attending to the precision necessary to solve the problem.

The ideas within the Mathematical Practices must be developed over time and throughout a student's K–12 school experience. During the primary grades, students can build an important foundation in which they begin to view mathematics as "more than completing sets of exercises or mimicking processes the teacher explains. Doing mathematics means generating strategies for solving problems, applying those approaches, seeing if they lead to solutions, and checking to see whether your answers make sense" (Van de Walle, Karp, & Bay-Williams, 2013, p. 13). When students view mathematics as interpreting, organizing, inquiring about, and constructing meaning, it becomes creative and alive (Fosnot & Dolk, 2001, p. 13).

Figure 7.9 Solving Number Stories Probe

1. Three students each solved the following problem.

Mike has 23 toy cars. Susan has 31 toy cars. How many more toy cars does Susan have than Mike?

Circle the name of the student you agree with. Use words or pictures to show your thinking.

2. Three students each solved the following problem.

Paula has some grapes. Carlos gave her 18 more grapes. Now Paula has 34 grapes. How many grapes did Paula have to start with?

Circle the name of the student you agree with. Use words or pictures to show your thinking.

Figure 7.10 Are They Equivalent? Probe Variation

Are They Equivalent?

1. Without adding the two numbers, use what you know about adding three-digit numbers to decide which of the number expressions below are equivalent to

$$427 + 569$$

	Circle One	Explain Your Answer
A. 724 + 965	Yes No	
B. 467 + 529	Yes No	
C. 527 + 469	Yes No	
D. 472 + 596	Yes No	
E. 927 + 69	Yes No	

2. Without subtracting, use what you know about subtracting three-digit numbers to decide which of the number expressions below are equivalent to

618 – 498

	Circle One	Explain Your Answer
A. 620 – 500	Yes No	
B. 681 – 489	Yes No	
C. 608 – 488	Yes No	
D. 698 – 418	Yes No	
E. 618 – 418 – 80	Yes No	

SHARING EXPERIENCES AND PROMOTING PROFESSIONAL COLLABORATION

The engine of improvement, growth, and renewal in a professional learning community is collective inquiry. The people in such a school are relentless in questioning the status quo, seeking new methods, testing those methods, and then reflecting on the results. ((DuFour, DuFour, Eaker, & Many, 2006, p. 68)

Using Probes provides an opportunity for collaboration among educators as they examine and discuss student work together:

The most important aspect of this strategy is that teachers have access to, and then develop for themselves the ability to understand, the content students are struggling with and ways that they, the teachers, can help. Pedagogical content knowledge—that special province of excellent teachers—is absolutely necessary for teachers to maximize their learning as they examine and discuss what students demonstrate they know and do not know. (Loucks-Horsley, Love, Stiles, Mundry, & Hewson, 2003, p. 183)

By providing research excerpts and instructional implications specific to the ideas of the Probe, the Teacher Notes can guide educators through the action research QUEST cycle, providing a collaborative framework for examining student thinking together and developing plans for improving instruction.

Our group of four first grade teachers meet during our lunch/specials block every other Tuesday to develop learning targets, talk about modifications and challenges for our lesson model, and determine common formative assessments to incorporate within our material. Sometimes the assessments are questions from the material itself, sometimes it is something we design ourselves, and sometimes we use a Probe.

Prior to using a Probe, we read through the Teacher Notes individually and come to the meeting with what stood out for us and any questions the Teacher Notes generated. After talking about the Teacher Notes, we then discuss how and when we would give the Probe. After giving the Probe, we discuss what we learned about our students and share student responses.

One particular Probe, the Value of the Digit, stands out for me because we were all surprised by the results. Even though the Teacher Notes indicated that students might circle 1 object when pointing to the 1 in the tens place, we were really confident that most of our students would circle 10 objects. Was I ever wrong! When we met to talk about the results, the others had also found that many more students circled 1 than we had anticipated. As we started reviewing our materials and upcoming targets, we realized that we needed to change the focus and language of some of the targets in order to better address the misconception.

As we continued throughout the unit, we were on a mission to revise our activities in order to provide opportunities for students to connect the meaning of the 1 in the tens place with the number of objects it represents. I came up with a new recording sheet for students to use during one of the games that I found helpful and enjoyed sharing with my colleagues.

The above instructional considerations provide information about how to use the Probes as a link between assessment, instruction, and learning. Embedded within each of the images from practice are several ideas for administering the Probes, including the following:

- Envelope for card sorts: Sums of Ten vignette p. 180
- Pictographs for displaying class data: Apples and Oranges vignette p. 183
- Sticky note reminders: Coloring One Half vignette, p. 179

SUMMARY

An important takeaway about using the Probes is the importance of your role in selecting and scaffolding Probes for use in the classroom. When selecting Probes, consider:

- how well the content of the Probe aligns to the targeted concepts you want students to learn;
- how well the structure of the Probe lends itself to the mathematical practice you wish students to incorporate; and
- how the Probe will serve as the link between assessment, instruction, and learning.

The first of the considerations, targeting the appropriate math content, was discussed in Chapter 1, where we outlined conceptual and procedural understanding and highlighted where in the Teacher Notes to find information about concepts targeted through a Probe. The second consideration, targeting the ideas within the practices, was the focus of this chapter. The final consideration, providing the link to learning, is a thread that runs throughout the book.

If you are new to using assessment Probes, we suggest that you try a couple of probes before returning to review the information in this chapter again after you have some firsthand experience. We also encourage you to visit uncoveringstudentideas.org to share experiences with others who are using Probes in mathematics and science. We look forward to hearing your ideas.

Appendix A

Information on the Standards for Mathematical Practice

The Standards for Mathematical Practice are not a checklist of teacher to-dos but rather support an environment in which the CCSS for mathematics content standards are enacted and are framed by specific expertise that you can use to help students develop their understanding and application of mathematics. (Larson et al., 2012, p. 26)

Formative assessment begins by identifying a learning goal, such as a grade-level expectation from the Common Core State Standards (CCSS). The Common Core State Standards for Mathematics (CCSSM) define what students should understand and be able to do in K–2 mathematics and beyond. Since the grade-level expectations in the CCSS define what students should "understand" or "be able to do," it is important for teachers to find out what students know and can do both conceptually and procedurally in relation to the expectation for learning.

In addition to these content standards, an important feature of the CCSSM is the Standards for Mathematical Practices. These practices describe a variety of processes, proficiencies, and dispositions that teachers at all grade levels should seek to develop in their students. Since the CCSSM do not define the methods and strategies used to determine the readiness and prior knowledge necessary to achieve the standards, the mathematics assessment Probes in this book complement CCSSM's eight Standards for Mathematical Practices and their link to mathematical content (Keeley & Rose Tobey, 2011, p. 30).

STRUCTURING THE MATHEMATICAL PRACTICE STANDARDS

Figure A.1   The Progression Project's Structure of the Mathematics Standards

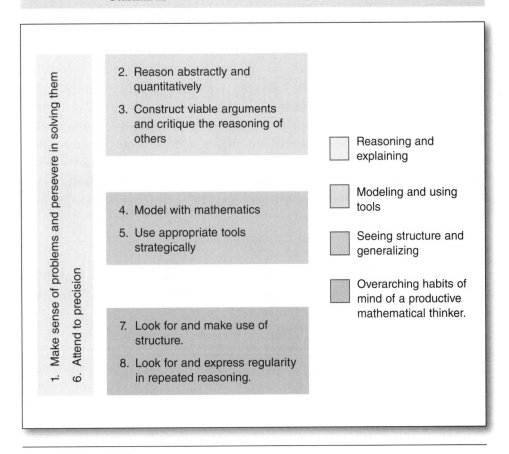

Source: McCallum (2011).

The Institute for Mathematics and Education's Progression Project is organizing the writing of final versions of the progressions documents for the K–12 Common Core State Standards. The work is being done by members of the original team along with mathematicians and educators not involved in the initial writing of the standards (Institute for Mathematics and Education, University of Arizona, 2007). The Progression Project created the diagram in Figure A.1 to provide some higher order structure to the practice standards, in the way that the clusters and domains provide higher order structure to the content standards.

The remaining part of this appendix will address each of the Practice Clusters using language from a variety of resources including the Common Core document (CCSSO, 2010) and the unpacking documents created by North Carolina's Department of Public Instruction (2012a, 2012b, 2012c). Following each of the descriptions of the practices within a cluster, we will describe how the Probes can be used in relationship to the ideas of each cluster. Included in these descriptions are images from practice that highlight various connections.

Reasoning and Explaining Practice Cluster (Practices 2 and 3)

Each of the Probes includes a Level 1 answer response and a Level 2 explanation prompt. These explanation prompts are the key to the practices within this Practice Cluster.

Mathematical Practice 2. Reason abstractly and quantitatively. Students demonstrate proficiency with this practice when they make sense of quantities and relationships while solving tasks. This involves both decontexualizing and contextualizing. When decontexualizing, students need to translate a situation into a number sentence that models the situation. When contextualizing, students need to pull from a task information to determine the mathematics required to solve the problem (CCSSO, 2010; North Carolina Department of Public Instruction, 2012a, 2012b, 2012c).

Students who reason abstractly and quantitatively are able to

- make sense of quantities and their relationships in problem situations.
- use quantitative reasoning that includes creating a coherent representation of the problem at hand.
- consider the units involved.
- attend to the meaning of quantities (not just how to compute them).
- know and flexibly use different properties of operations and objects.
- use abstract reasoning when measuring and comparing the lengths of objects.

Mathematical Practice 3. Construct viable arguments and critique the reasoning of others. Students demonstrate proficiency with this practice when they accurately use mathematical terms to construct arguments, engage in discussions about problem-solving strategies, examine a variety of problem-solving strategies, and begin to recognize the reasonableness of them, as well as similarities and differences among them (CCSSO, 2010; North Carolina Department of Public Instruction, 2012a, 2012b, 2012c).

Students who construct viable arguments and critique the reasoning of others are able to

- make conjectures and build a logical progression of statements to explore the truth of their conjectures.
- recognize and use counterexamples.
- justify their conclusions, communicate them to others, and respond to the arguments of others.
- distinguish correct logic or reasoning from that which is flawed and, if there is a flaw in an argument, explain what it is.
- construct arguments using concrete referents such as objects, drawings, diagrams, and actions. (In the lower grades, such arguments can

make sense and be correct, even though they are not generalized or made formal until later grades.)

- listen to or read the arguments of others, decide whether they make sense, and ask useful questions to clarify or improve arguments.

SEEING STRUCTURE AND GENERALIZING PRACTICE CLUSTER (PRACTICES 7 AND 8)

Young children make sense of their world by looking for patterns and structure and routines. They learn by integrating new information into cognitive structures they have developed, and they are naturally curious and eager to explore new ideas. Young learners are the perfect candidates for this practice cluster.

Mathematical Practice 7. Look for and make use of structure. Students demonstrate proficiency with this practice when they look for patterns and structures in the number system and other areas of mathematics such as modeling problems involving types of operations. Examples of patterns and structures within the number system include recognition that the commutative property holds for addition but not for subtraction and making use of place value ideas to decompose and recompose numbers in multiple ways. By seeking contextual structures and problem types—including "result unknown," "change unknown," and "start unknown," students begin to generalize a model for solving each type of problem (CCSSO, 2010; North Carolina Department of Public Instruction, 2012a, 2012b, 2012c).

Students who look for and make use of structure are able to

- notice that 3 and 7 more is the same amount as 7 and 3 more.
- sort a collection of shapes according to how many sides the shapes have.
- see things as single objects or as being composed of several objects. (For example, kindergarten students are able to view the number 10 as a single quantity but also as 10 ones.)

Mathematical Practice 8. Look for and express regularity in repeated reasoning. Students demonstrate proficiency with this practice when they look for regularity in problem structures when problem solving, notice if calculations are repeated, and look both for general methods and for shortcuts, for example, noticing that $4 + 4 + 4$ is the same as 4×3. Students are able to compose and decompose numbers in systematic ways, for example, to find all the different pairs of numbers that add to a given sum (CCSSO, 2010; North Carolina Department of Public Instruction, 2012a, 2012b, 2012c).

Students who look for and express regularity in repeated reasoning are able to

- notice if calculations are repeated.
- look both for general methods and for shortcuts.
- continually evaluate the reasonableness of their intermediate results.

MODELING AND USING TOOLS PRACTICE CLUSTER (PRACTICES 4 AND 5)

Students use multiple different tools (e.g., rulers, counters, base-ten blocks, calculators, etc.) in the primary mathematics classroom. How the tools are used depends on the mathematics topic of focus, and the same tool might be used in a variety of contexts. When given a problem, students need to be able to determine what tool would be appropriate, how the tool could be used in solving the problem, and how to communicate about their process. In the early grades, students are often using tools to model a problem. It is also important for students to be able to communicate about the modeling process by representing the process using numbers and symbols.

Mathematical Practice 4. Model with mathematics. Students demonstrate proficiency with this practice when they model real-life mathematical situations with a number sentence or an equation and check to make sure that their equation accurately matches the problem context. Young students often rely on concrete manipulatives and pictorial representations while solving tasks, but the expectation is that they will also write an equation to model problem situations. For example, while solving the story problem, "There are 6 apples on the counter. If you eat 2 apples, how many are left?" kindergarten students are expected to write the equation $6 - 2 = 4$. Likewise, primary students are expected to create an appropriate problem situation from an equation. For example, students are expected to create a story problem for the equation $35 + 28 = $ ___ such as, "There were 35 pennies in the jar. Tom added 28 more pennies. How many pennies are now in the jar?" (CCSSO, 2010; North Carolina Department of Public Instruction, 2012a, 2012b, 2012c).

Students who model with mathematics are able to

- apply what they know to make approximations.
- identify important quantities in a problem situation.
- analyze relationships between quantities.
- reflect on whether the results make sense.

Mathematical Practice 5. Use appropriate tools strategically. Students demonstrate proficiency with this practice when they access and use tools appropriately. These tools may include counters, place value (base-ten) blocks, hundreds charts, number lines, and concrete geometric shapes (e.g., pattern blocks, 3-D solids) and measurement tools. Students should also have experiences with educational technologies, such as calculators, and virtual manipulatives that support conceptual understanding. During classroom instruction, students should have access to various mathematical tools as well as paper and pencil, and determine which tools are the most appropriate to use. Grade K–2 students are expected to explain why they used specific mathematical tools. For example, while measuring the length of the hallway, students should be able to explain why a yardstick is more appropriate to use than a ruler (CCSSO, 2010; North Carolina Department of Public Instruction, 2012a, 2012b, 2012c).

Students who use appropriate tools strategically are able to

- consider available tools when solving a mathematical problem.
- select tools to match their problem-solving needs.
- explain their choice of a particular tool for a given problem.
- detect possible errors by reasoning about whether their answer makes sense.

OVERARCHING HABITS OF MIND OF PRODUCTIVE THINKERS PRACTICE CLUSTER (PRACTICES 1 AND 6)

Productive disposition refers to the tendency to see sense in mathematics, to perceive it as both useful and worthwhile, to believe that steady effort in learning mathematics pays off, and to see oneself as an effective learner and doer of mathematics. Developing a productive disposition requires frequent opportunities to make sense of mathematics, to recognize the benefits of perseverance, and to experience the rewards of sense making in mathematics. (Donovan & Bransford, 2005, p. 131)

Mathematical Practice 1. Make sense and persevere in solving problems. Students demonstrate proficiency with this practice when they make sense of the meaning of the task and find an entry point or a way to start the task. Grade K–2 students also develop a foundation for problem-solving strategies and become independently proficient in using those strategies to solve new tasks. Students use concrete manipulatives and pictorial representations as well as mental mathematics. Students also are expected to persevere while solving tasks; that is, if students reach a point in which they are stuck, they can think about the task in a different way and continue working toward a solution. Mathematically proficient students determine whether their solutions are complete by asking themselves the question, "Does my answer make sense?" If they determine the answer doesn't make sense, they look for where the error occurred (CCSSO, 2010; North Carolina Department of Public Instruction, 2012a, 2012b, 2012c).

Students who use appropriate tools strategically are able to

- start by explaining to themselves the meaning of a problem and looking for entry points to its solution.
- make conjectures about a solution.
- plan a solution pathway rather than simply jumping into a solution attempt.
- monitor and evaluate their progress and change course if necessary.
- use concrete objects or pictures to help conceptualize and solve a problem.
- check their answers to problems using a different method.
- routinely ask themselves, "Does this make sense?"
- make sense of the problem-solving approaches of others, noticing similarities and differences among approaches.

Mathematical Practice 6. Attend to precision. Students demonstrate proficiency with this practice when they are precise in their communication, calculations, and measurements. In all mathematical tasks, students in grades K–2 communicate clearly, using grade-level appropriate vocabulary accurately. During tasks involving number sense, students consider whether their answer is reasonable and check their work to ensure the accuracy of solutions. When measuring or using measurement data, students know that measures must include a number and a unit and are able to specify what unit is appropriate (CCSSO, 2010; North Carolina Department of Public Instruction, 2012a, 2012b, 2012c).

Students who attend to precision are able to

- communicate precisely to others.
- use clear definitions in discussion with others and in their own reasoning.
- state the meaning of the symbols they choose, including using the equal sign consistently and appropriately.
- carefully specify units of measurement to clarify their correspondence with quantities in a problem.
- give carefully formulated explanations to other students.
- communicate precisely to others by providing details and/or examples to support their ideas.
- use informal and formal definitions when sharing their thinking with others.
- state the meaning of the symbols they choose, including using the equal sign consistently and appropriately.
- specify units of measurement to describe quantities in a problem.
- share their explanations with other students.

Chapter 7 covers more about how the Probes support teachers in assessing ideas related to the mathematical practices.

Appendix B

Developing Assessment Probes

Developing an assessment Probe is different from creating appropriate questions for comprehensive diagnostic assessments and summative measures of understanding. The Probes in this book were developed using a process similar to that described in *Mathematics Curriculum Topic Study: Bridging the Gap Between Standards and Practice* (Keeley & Rose, 2006) and the accompanying *Facilitator's Guide* (Mundry, Keeley, & Rose Tobey, 2012).

The process is summarized as follows:

• Use national standards to examine concepts and specific ideas related to a topic. The national standards used to develop the Probes for this book are the Common Core Standards for Mathematics (CCSSO, 2010). The Common Core State Standards for Mathematics (CCSSM) define what students should understand and be able to do in K–12 mathematics.

• Within a CCSSM grade-level expectation, select the specific concepts or ideas you plan to address, and identify the relevant research findings. Sources for research findings include the *Research Companion to Principles and Standards for School Mathematics* (NCTM, 2003), *Elementary and Middle School Mathematics: Teaching Developmentally* (Van de Walle, Karp, & Bay-Williams, 2013), articles from NCTM's *Journal for Research in Mathematics Education* and its *Second Handbook of Research on Mathematics Teaching and Learning* (2007), and additional supplemental articles related to the topic.

• Focus on a concept or a specific idea you plan to address with the Probe, and identify the related research findings. Keep the targeted concept small enough to assess within a few items, as Probes are meant to be administered in a short amount of time. Rather than trying to target as much information about a topic as possible, it is better to be more narrow and focused.

- Choose the type of Probe format that lends itself to the situation. (See more information on Probe format in the section that follows.) Develop the stem (the prompt), key (correct response), and distractors (incorrect responses derived from research findings) that match the developmental level of your students.

- Share your assessment Probe(s) with colleagues for constructive feedback, pilot with students, and modify as needed.

Feedback on the assessment Probes developed for this resource was collected from K–2 educators across multiple states, and the Probes were piloted with students across multiple grade levels. The feedback and student work were used to revise the Probes and to support the development of the accompanying Teacher Notes.

Appendix C
Action Research Reflection Template

QUEST Cycle

Questions to Consider About the Key Mathematical Concepts

What is the concept you wish to target? Is the concept at grade level, or is it a prerequisite?

Uncovering Student Understanding About the Key Concepts

How will you collect information from students (e.g., paper and pencil, interview, student response system, etc.)? What form will you use (e.g., one-page Probe, card sort, etc.)? Are there adaptations you plan to make? Review the summary of typical student responses.

Exploring Excerpts From Educational Resources and Related Research

Review the quotes from research about common difficulties related to the Probe. What do you predict to be common understandings and/or misunderstandings for your students?

Surveying the Prompts and Selected Responses in the Probe

Sort by selected responses; then re-sort by patterns in thinking. What common understandings/misunderstandings did the Probe elicit? How do these elicited understanding/misunderstandings compare to those listed in the Teacher Notes?

Teaching Implications and Considerations

Review the bulleted list, and decide how you will take action. What actions did you take? How did you assess the impact of those actions? What are your next steps?

References

Ashlock, R. B. (2006). *Error patterns in computation.* Upper Saddle River, NJ: Pearson.

Askew, M., & Wiliam, D. (1995). *Recent research in mathematics education 5–16.* London, UK: HMSO.

Bamberger, H., Oberdorf, C., & Schulz-Farrell, K. (2010). *Math misconceptions: From misunderstanding to deep understanding.* Portsmouth, NH: Heinemann.

Bay Area Mathematics Task Force. (1999). *A mathematics sourcebook for elementary and middle school teachers.* Novato, CA: Arena Press.

Black, P., & Harrison, C. (2004). *Science inside the black box: Assessment for learning in the science classroom.* London, UK: NFER/Nelson.

Black, P., Harrison C., Lee, C., Marshall, B., & Wiliam, D. (2004). Working inside the black box: Assessment for learning in the classroom. *Phi Delta Kappan, 86*(1), 8–21.

Burns, M. (2005). Looking at how students reason. *Educational Leadership: Assessment to Promote Learning, 63*(3), 26–31.

Cain, C., & Faulkner, V. (2011). Teaching number in the early elementary years. *Teaching Children Mathematics, 18*(5), 288–295.

Clements, D., & Sarama, J. (2004). *Engaging young children in mathematics: Standards for early childhood mathematics education.* Mahwah, NJ: Lawrence Erlbaum.

Clements, D., & Sarama, J. (2007). Early childhood mathematics learning. In F. K. Lester, Jr. (Ed.), *Second handbook of research on mathematics teaching and learning* (pp. 461–555). New York, NY: Information Age.

Clements, D., & Sarama, J. (2009). *Learning and teaching early math: The learning trajectories approach.* New York, NY: Routledge.

Copley, J. V., Glass, K., Nix, L., Faseler, A., De Jesus, M., & Tanksley, S. (2004). Measuring experiences for young children. *Teaching Children Mathematics, 10*(6), 314–319.

Common Core Standards Writing Team. (2011a). *Progressions for the Common Core State Standards in Mathematics (draft): K, counting and cardinality.* Retrieved from http://ime.math.arizona.edu/progressions/#products

Common Core Standards Writing Team. (2011b). *Progressions for the Common Core State Standards in Mathematics (draft): K–3, categorical data; grades 2–5, Measurement Data.* Retrieved from http://ime.math.arizona.edu/progressions/#products

Common Core Standards Writing Team. (2011c). *Progressions for the Common Core State Standards in Mathematics (draft): K–5, number and operations in base ten.* Retrieved from http://ime.math.arizona.edu/progressions/#products

Common Core Standards Writing Team. (2011d). *Progressions for the Common Core State Standards in Mathematics (draft): K–5, operations and algebraic thinking.* Retrieved from http://ime.math.arizona.edu/progressions/#products

Common Core Standards Writing Team. (2012a). *Progressions for the Common Core State Standards in Mathematics (draft): K–5, Geometric measurement.* Retrieved from http://ime.math.arizona.edu/progressions/#products

Common Core Standards Writing Team. (2012b). *Progressions for the Common Core State Standards in Mathematics (draft): K–6, geometry.* Retrieved from http:// ime.math.arizona.edu/progressions/#products

Council of Chief State School Officers (CCSSO). (2008). *Attributes of effective formative assessment.* Retrieved from http://www.ccsso.org/publications/details .cfm?PublicationID=362

Council of Chief State School Officers (CCSSO). (2010). *Common core state standards.* Retrieved from http://corestandards.org

Dacey, L., & Collins, A. (2010). *Zeroing in on number and operations: Key ideas and misconceptions, Grades 1–2.* Portland, ME: Stenhouse.

Dietiker, L. C., Gonulates, F., & Smith, J. (2011). Understanding linear measure. *Teaching Children Mathematics, 18*(4), 252–259.

Donovan, S., & Bransford, J. (2005). *How students learn mathematics in the classroom.* Washington, DC: National Academies Press.

DuFour, R., DuFour, R, Eaker, R., & Many, T. (2006). *Learning by doing: A handbook for professional learning communities at work.* Bloomington, IN: Solution Tree.

Empson, S. B. (1999). Equal sharing and shared meaning: The development of fraction concepts in a first-grade classroom. *Cognition and Instruction, 17*(3), 283–342.

Falkner, K., Levi, L., & Carpenter, T. (1999). Children's understanding of equality: A foundation for algebra. *Teaching Children Mathematics, 5,* 232–236.

Fosnot, C., & Dolk, M. (2001). *Young mathematicians at work: Constructing number sense, addition, and subtraction.* Portsmouth, NH: Heinemann.

Friel, S. N., Curcio, F. R., & Bright, G. W. (2001). Making sense of graphs: Critical factors influencing comprehension and instructional implications. *Journal for Research in Mathematics Education, 32*(2).

Garcia, L. (2012). *How to get students talking! Generating math talk that supports math learning.* Retrieved from http://www.mathsolutions.com/documents/How_ to_Get_Students_Talking.pdf

Gelman, R., & Gallistel, C. R. (1978). *The child's understanding of number.* Cambridge, MA: Harvard University Press.

Gersten, R., Beckmann, S., Clarke, B., Foegen, A., Marsh, L., Star, J. R., & Witzel, B. (2009). *Assisting students struggling with mathematics: Response to Intervention (RTI) for elementary and middle schools* (NCEE 2009-4060). Retrieved from http://ies.ed.gov/ncee/wwc/practiceguide.aspx?sid=2

Hanich, L. B., Jordan, N. C., Kaplan, D., & Dick, J. (2001). Performance across different areas of mathematical cognition in children with learning difficulties. *Journal of Educational Psychology, 93,* 615–626.

Heritage, M. (2010). *Formative assessment: Making it happen in the classroom.* Thousand Oaks, CA: Corwin.

Hiebert, J., & Wearne, D. (1992). Links between teaching and learning place value with understanding in first grade. *Journal for Research in Mathematical Education, 23*(2), 98–122.

Institute for Mathematics and Education, University of Arizona. (2007). *Progressions documents for the common core math standards: About this project.* Retrieved from http://math.arizona.edu/~ime/progressions/

Jensen, R. J. (1993). *Research ideas for the classroom: Early childhood mathematics.* New York, NY: MacMillan.

Kamii, C. (1986). Place value: An explanation of its difficulty and educational implications for the primary grades. *Journal of Research in Childhood Education, 1*(2), 75–86.

Keeley, P. (2012, April). Misunderstanding misconceptions. *Science Scope,* 12–15.

Keeley, P., & Rose, C. (2006). *Mathematics curriculum topic study: Bridging the gap between standards and practice.* Thousand Oaks, CA: Corwin.

Keeley, P., & Rose Tobey, C. (2011). *Mathematics formative assessment: 75 practical strategies for linking assessment, instruction and learning.* Thousand Oaks, CA: Corwin.

Larson, M., Fennell, F., Lott Adams, T., Dixon, J. K., Kobett, B. M., Wray, J. A., & Kanold, T. (2012). *Common Core mathematics in a PLC at work: Grades K–2.* Bloomington, IN: Solution Tree.

Littler, G. H., & Jirotková, D. (2008). Primary school pupils' misconceptions in number. *Supporting Independent Thinking Through Mathematical Education, 55,* 55–60.

Loucks-Horsley, S., Love, N., Stiles, K., Mundry, S., & Hewson, P. (2003). *Designing professional development for teachers of science and mathematics.* Thousand Oaks, CA: Corwin.

McCallum, B. (2011, March 10). Structuring the mathematical practices [Web log post]. Retrieved from http://commoncoretools.me/2011/03/10/structuring-the-mathematical-practices/

McManus, S. M. (2008). *Attributes of effective formative assessment.* Washington, DC: Council of Chief State School Officers.

McTighe, J., & O'Connor, K. (2005). Seven practices for effective learning. *Educational Leadership: Assessment to Promote Learning, 63*(3), 10–17.

Mestre, J. (1989). *Hispanic and Anglo students' misconceptions in mathematics.* Charleston, WV: Appalachia Educational Laboratory. Retrieved from ERIC database (ED313192).

Minton, L. (2007). *What if your ABCs were your 123s? Building connections between literacy and numeracy.* Thousand Oaks, CA: Corwin.

Mundry, S., Keeley, P., & Rose Tobey, C. (2012). *Facilitator's guide to mathematics curriculum topic study.* Thousand Oaks, CA: Corwin.

National Council of Teachers of Mathematics (NCTM). (2000). *Principles and standards for school mathematics.* Reston, VA: Author.

National Council of Teachers of Mathematics. (2001). *K–2 navigating geometry.* Reston, VA: Author.

National Council of Teachers of Mathematics. (2003). *Research companion to principles and standards for school mathematics.* Reston, VA: Author.

National Research Council (NRC). (2001). *Adding it up: Helping children learn mathematics.* Washington, DC: National Academies Press.

National Research Council (NRC). (2005). *How students learn mathematics in the classroom.* Washington, DC: National Academies Press.

Naylor, S., & Keogh, B. (2000). *Concept cartoons in science education.* Sandbach, UK: Millgate House Education.

North Carolina Department of Public Instruction. (2012a). *Instructional support tools for achieving new standards: K grade mathematics unpacked content.* Retrieved from http://www.ncpublicschools.org/acre/standards/common-core-tools/#unmath

North Carolina Department of Public Instruction. (2012b). *Instructional support tools for achieving new standards: 1st grade mathematics unpacked content.* Retrieved from http://www.ncpublicschools.org/acre/standards/common-core-tools/#unmath

North Carolina Department of Public Instruction. (2012c). *Instructional support tools for achieving new standards: 2nd grade mathematics unpacked content.* Retrieved from http://www.ncpublicschools.org/acre/standards/common-core-tools/#unmath

Oberdorf, C. D., & Taylor-Cox, J. (1999). Shape up! *Teaching Children Mathematics, 5*(6), 340–342.

Razel, M., & Eylon, B.-S. (1991, June/July). *Developing mathematics readiness in young children with the Agam Program.* Fifteenth Conference of the International Group for the Psychology of Mathematics Education, Assisi, Italy.

Resnick, L. (1983). Mathematics and science learning: A new conception. *Science, 220,* 477–478.

Rose, C., & Arline, C. (2009). *Uncovering student thinking in mathematics, grades 6–12: 30 formative assessment probes for the secondary classroom.* Thousand Oaks, CA: Corwin.

Rose, C., Minton, L., & Arline, C. (2007). *Uncovering student thinking in mathematics: 25 formative assessment probes.* Thousand Oaks, CA: Corwin.

Rose Tobey, C., & Minton, L. (2011). *Uncovering student thinking in mathematics grades K–5: 25 formative assessment probes for the elementary classroom.* Thousand Oaks, CA: Corwin.

Ross, S. (1989). Parts, wholes and place value: A developmental view. *Arithmetic Teacher, 36*(6), 47–51.

Rowley, C., Gervasoni, A., Clarke, D., Horne, M., & McDonough, A. (2001, September). *Early numeracy research project (ENRP): Using interviews to monitor growth in mathematics.* Paper presented to the British Educational Research Association Annual Conference, University of Leeds, 13–15 September.

Ryan, J., & Williams, J. (2007). *Children's mathematics 4–15.* Berkshire, UK: Open University Press.

Schaeffer, B., Eggleston, V., & Scott, J. (1974). Number development in young children. *Cognitive Psychology, 6,* 357–379.

Siebert, D., & Gaskin, N. (2006). Creating, naming, and justifying fractions. *Teaching Children Mathematics, 12*(8), 394–400.

Siegler, R., Carpenter, T., Fennell, F., Geary, D., Lewis, J., Okamoto . . . Wray, J. (2010). *Developing effective fractions instruction for kindergarten through 8th grade.* NCEE 2010-4039. Retrieved from http://ies.ed.gov/ncee/wwc/practiceguide .aspx?sid=15

Small, M. (2009). *Good questions: Great ways to differentiate mathematics instruction.* New York, NY: Teachers College Press.

Sowder, J. L., & Nickerson, S. (2010). *Reconceptualizing mathematics for elementary school teachers.* Boston, MA: W. H. Freeman.

Stepans, J. I., Schmidt, D. L., Welsh, K. M., Reins, K. J., & Saigo, B. W. (2005). *Teaching for K–12 mathematical understanding using the conceptual change model.* St. Cloud, MN: Saiwood.

Thompson, C., & Siegler, R. (2010). Linear numerical-magnitude representations aid children's memory for numbers. *Psychological Science, 21,* 1274–1281.

Van de Walle, J. A. (2007). *Elementary and middle school mathematics* (6th ed.). Boston, MA: Pearson.

Van de Walle, J. A., Karp, K., & Bay-Williams, J. (2013). *Elementary and middle school mathematics* (8th ed.). Boston, MA: Pearson.

Van Den Brink, J. (1984). Acoustic counting and quantity counting. *For the Learning of Mathematics, (4)*2, 2–13.

Watson, B., & Konicek, R. (1990). Teaching for conceptual change: Confronting children's experience. *Phi Delta Kappan, 71*(9), 680–684.

Weiland, L. (2007). Experiences to help children learn to count on. *Teaching Children Mathematics, 14*(3), 188–192.

Wiliam, D. (2011). *Embedded formative assessment.* Bloomington, IN: Solution Tree.

Wylie, E., Gullickson, A. R., Cummings, K. E., Egelson, P. E., Noakes, L. A., Norman, K. M., & Veeder, S. A. (2012). *Improving formative assessment practice to empower student learning.* Thousand Oaks, CA: Corwin.

Yetkin, E. (2003). *Student difficulties in learning elementary mathematics.* ERIC Clearinghouse for Science Mathematics and Environmental Education. (Document Reproduction Service No. Retrieved from ERIC database (ED482727).

Index

CORWIN

A SAGE Company

The Corwin logo—a raven striding across an open book—represents the union of courage and learning. Corwin is committed to improving education for all learners by publishing books and other professional development resources for those serving the field of PreK–12 education. By providing practical, hands-on materials, Corwin continues to carry out the promise of its motto: **"Helping Educators Do Their Work Better."**